The Ten-Minute Gardener's Flower-Growing Diary

Val Bourne

in association with
The Daily Telegraph

BANTAM PRESS

LONDON • TORONTO • SYDNEY • AUCKLAND • JOHANNESBURG

TRANSWORLD PUBLISHERS
61–63 Uxbridge Road, London W5 5SA
A Random House Group Company
www.transworldbooks.co.uk

First published in Great Britain
in 2011 by Bantam Press
an imprint of Transworld Publishers

A CIP catalogue record for this book
is available from the British Library.

ISBN 9780593066683

Addresses for Random House Group Ltd companies outside the UK
can be found at: www.randomhouse.co.uk
The Random House Group Ltd Reg. No. 954009

The Random House Group Limited supports the Forest Stewardship Council (FSC®), the leading international forest-certification organization. Our books carrying the FSC label are printed on FSC®-certified paper. FSC is the only forest-certification scheme endorsed by the leading environmental organizations, including Greenpeace. Our paper-procurement policy can be found at www.randomhouse.co.uk/environment.

Typeset in Weiss and Mrs Eaves by Falcon Oast Graphic Art Ltd.
Printed and bound in Great Britain by
CPI Group (UK) Ltd, Croydon, CR0 4YY

2 4 6 8 10 9 7 5 3 1

FSC www.fsc.org MIX Paper from responsible sources FSC® C016897

To the Best Beloved, for his helpful marginalia

CONTENTS

ACKNOWLEDGEMENTS

Thank you to Susanna Wadeson for her enthusiastic help and support, without which I would have gone under!

Thank you to Brenda Updegraff for her very necessary, eagle-eyed editing. Thank you to Andrew Davidson for the cover illustration and to Patrick Mulrey for the illustrations inside.

Thank you to Tom Poland and to Philip Lord for the design.

And thank you to my family for their patience over the long months.

PREFACE

THIS FLOWER-GROWING diary aims to explain the mysteries of what to plant, when to plant, when to divide and how to propagate, so the novice gardener should find it invaluable. However, it isn't written just for the beginner: this little book contains all the information I've amassed over decades of growing flowers in my own garden. I hope that even the most experienced gardener will find plenty to fascinate. I've chosen the very best varieties and, as a member of the RHS trials panel for dahlias and perennials, I do get to see the cream of the crop.

It's also written for the gardener of today and the approach is entirely organic. If you select excellent varieties (and satisfy their individual needs by planting them in the right place) your plants will remain healthy and disease-free without chemical intervention. It may mean compromises. The gardener with light soil in a dry county may not manage moisture-demanding phloxes, for example, but will triumph with sparkling silvers instead.

I hope this diary inspires you. I have tried to go beyond the 'dig a hole and plant it 2 feet deep' advice and evoke what my garden is for me. I have been lucky enough to have been in the gentle world of gardening since the age of three or four. It has never lost its charm, nor will it.

Val Bourne

JANUARY

The days are stretching out, but the sun has little strength and it will be late February before it's possible to feel any warmth from overhead. At this time of year the gardener must be governed by the weather, because January can be cold and bleak in some years and mild and damp in others.

At some point in the next 6 weeks late-season plants and grasses should be cut back. Once that happens it's possible to begin to tidy up and weed. If it is mild, this is your main task, but in a cold year bide your time and wait.

Otherwise, organize yourself for the coming months. Straight after Christmas garden centres stock up for the year ahead and you can buy everything you need. By spring supplies can be thin on the ground.

1 Snow Damage
(early January)

GARDENS at this time of year are often covered by a layer of snow. This is good news for some plants and bad news for others. Snow definitely protects perennials that have retreated underground from harsh temperatures. It suits bulbs too: they generally welcome the snow melt once better weather arrives. Lots of herbaceous plants also shine after a period of really cold weather. It keeps them dormant and allows them to rest properly. Peonies, roses and tulips always shine more brightly after a cold winter.

Evergreen plants lying under snow are the most vulnerable. They can be damaged by the sheer weight, which seems to increase once a thaw sets in. It's better to knock snow down as soon as it arrives on these plants and hedges – a rake or broom handle is a good weapon for the job. Some conifers or hedges might have become misshapen already if the snow was wet when it fell, but if you bind them up with garden twine and canes and leave them alone for 3–6 months you can usually reshape them. Check all your evergreens once the weather improves and remove any damaged branches.

You will have to be careful where you walk if there's a blanket of snow because it's easy to stray off the lawn and snap a plant hidden under snow when you can't see what's where. So enjoy the view from inside by the fire, or get the sledge out. Gardening and snow are completely incompatible.

Did you know? Wet snow is much denser and does far more damage than fine, dry snow. On average, 25cm (10in) of snow weighs as much as 2.5cm (1in) of rain, but wet snow, although it forms a thinner layer, is twice as dense.

Organic Tip ✔

If you have evergreen topiary or hedges in the garden, try to prune them regularly so that they stay bushy and compact. Then they will hold their shape well in snow and also provide a snug refuge for hibernating insects.

SECRETS OF OVERWINTERING SUCCESS

- Mulch vulnerable plants in the garden (alstroemerias, agapanthus and left-in-the-ground dahlias, etc.) with a thick layer of bark applied in November.
- Dry off potted plants (like agapanthus) in September, then move them close to the house or put them in the greenhouse to prevent heavy rain from soaking the roots. Laying pots on their sides also keeps them drier.
- Always use thick, frost-proof pots for permanent containers. Terracotta is the warmest.
- Thick horticultural fleece can make the difference between life and death, both outside and in the greenhouse.
- Take insurance cuttings of vulnerable plants like salvias, ballotas and penstemons.
- Do most of your herbaceous cutting down in early spring if you can. The top growth protects the root-stocks in winter.
- Should you appear to have lost something, allow it time to return. Don't write it off until mid-July because plants do come back from the depths – but it takes a long time.

2 Check Tools and Sundries

(early January)

GARDENING will be off the agenda in January, but often the gardener is raring to go. So turn your attention to maintaining the tools of your trade. All wooden-handled tools should have a coating of raw linseed oil to feed the wood. It will help to preserve your tools and give the wood a silky feel. Wipe over stainless steel (a wonderful material for trowels and spades) with a soft, clean cloth – remember to brush the mud off first.

Book the mower in for a service before it gets busy.

Check your supplies of labels, seed trays, canes and string. January is the month when garden centres groan with garden sundries and, if you buy them before the spring rush, you should find everything you need.

It's also a good time to clean seed trays and small pots ready for seed sowing. Cleanliness is important because it prevents fungal diseases. Make sure watering cans are in a clean and sound condition. A good can with a fine rose is a necessity, albeit an expensive one. Taken care of, it can outlive you. Go through all your seeds and buy any that you need. Order dahlia tubers and other summer bulbs.

Did you know? Garden tools have hardly changed in centuries. The Romans established the pattern for the spades and shovels that we still use today when they harnessed the technology of the forge to heat iron to its malleable point. In the mid-fourteenth century iron-smelting made it possible to create lighter, more precisely shaped tools. When the Industrial Revolution came, steel and alloys led to the manufacture of tools that were lighter, finer and far more durable.

Organic Tip ✔

Don't buy tools on the internet. Always handle a tool before you buy it and check that it's not too heavy and clumsy. Check the quality and make sure it's balanced – that you can pick it up in one hand without it being too heavy at one end. Try to buy a tool that will last you for decades, not a cheap alternative.

3 Buy a Hamamelis to Brighten January

(mid-January)

THIS IS the very best time to buy a hamamelis, or witch hazel, because they are in flower in garden centres and nurseries now. It is important to buy them in bloom because flower quality, colour and scent vary enormously. It's also unwise to go by the name on the label: sadly, many are incorrect.

Witch hazels can be grown by most gardeners who have fertile soil. They are not acid-lovers, but they do need moisture, especially in summer. Those gardening on chalk soil will struggle unless they can improve an area of ground with organic matter.

The spidery flowers come in marmalade, citrus and chilli colours and their ribbons shrug off wintry weather brilliantly. Scent varies between freesia and lavatory cleaner, so do sniff them well if scent is important to you. The ribbons are held in large calyces and sometimes these are bright red, adding to the overall vibrance. Foliage is hazel-like but it also varies. Some leaves have a crinkle-cut crisp look. Several varieties colour up in autumn to a brilliant red, but not all.

By the time the witch hazels drop their leaves, fist-like clusters of buds are clearly visible. The fact that these shrubs flower reliably in January makes them unique. Because the weather does not affect their flowers, they always flower in January, whereas other shrubs are held back by bad weather.

Hamamelis need warm summer sun to ripen their wood and encourage flower buds, so dank, dark corners are not suitable. Also, a warm position ensures that any of that subtle scent pervades the air. So if you think you can grow one, seek one out in January. Be prepared to pay. These grafted, slow-growing shrubs (which usually have a branching shape) are expensive.

Did you know? Hamamelis are found in North America and parts of Asia, which were once the same landmass. When the two continents drifted apart American witch hazels evolved differently from their Asian cousins. When twentieth-century plant collectors introduced the Asian species into America the two hybridized naturally. These interspecific hybrids, known as *Hamamelis × intermedia*, were greatly improved by the de Belder family at the Kalmthout Arboretum in Belgium. Buy forms of *Hamamelis × intermedia* because their flowers are much larger.

Organic Tip ✔

Summer moisture is the key to growing hamamelis. Water them well in dry summers by gently tipping a couple of buckets of water over their roots at least once a week. Mulching with bark in spring also helps – but make sure that the soil is warm and wet first. If using bark, add a sprinkling of blood, fish and bone (a slow-release fertilizer) or powdered chicken manure.

SECRETS OF SUCCESS

- Good fertile soil, summer moisture and a reasonably open situation are necessities.
- Don't prune hard. These shrubs are slow-growing. Tip the branches and slightly shorten the side shoots after flowering if necessary.
- Don't crowd them with other plants. Use spring-flowering bulbs, as these die down by summer, allowing the hamamelis to get all the rain going.
- Buy in January and plant in suitable conditions in well-enriched ground.
- If you see the leaves turn sharply downwards in summer, this indicates drought stress. Water immediately.

VARIETIES OF *HAMAMELIS* x *INTERMEDIA*

'Pallida' AGM
Citrus-lemon flowers with a freesia scent. Yellow autumn leaves. The best sulphur-yellow witch hazel.

'Aurora' AGM
Butterscotch-orange flowers with a strong freesia scent. Yellow autumn leaves.

'Aphrodite' AGM
Strong, thick, orange-red ribbons held in purplish calyces. A unique colour. A faint scent and yellow autumn leaves.

'Diane' AGM
Best red-flowered form, with large red ribbons. A slight scent and good autumn colour.

'Vesna' AGM
The strongly fragrant, twisted flowers are a fiery blend of orange-yellow and red. In autumn the foliage colours up well to red.

'Barmstedt Gold' AGM
Golden-yellow flowers, neatly arranged, with a medium-sweet scent. Yellow autumn leaves.

4 Cut Natural Stakes

(mid-January)

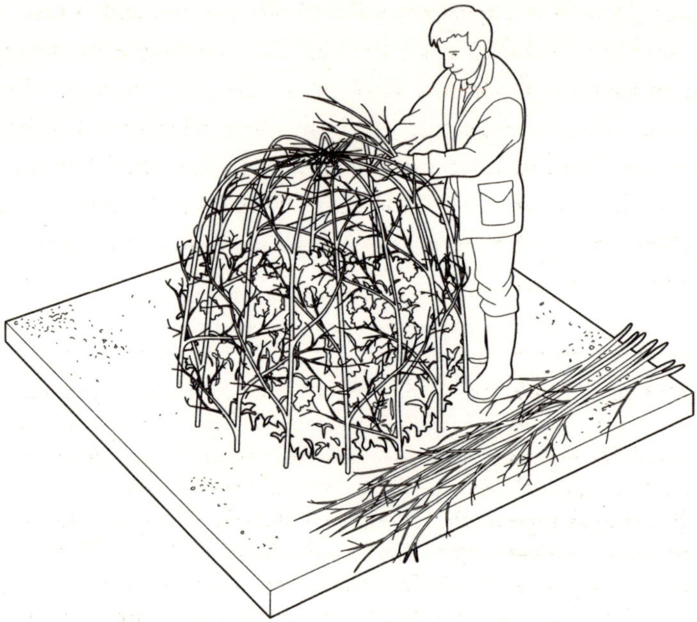

JANUARY is also an excellent month to sort out materials for plant-staking, and going natural looks so much better than using smooth bamboo canes. Cutting some hazel rods from a wood (with the owner's permission) every year is a necessity because natural stakes last only 1–2 years. You will also need to collect twiggy sticks 90–120cm (3–4ft) long to use as pea sticks. Also look out for sturdier branches with a Y-shaped end similar to a catapult. These make excellent dahlia supports.

Hazel twigs are the most useful for staking and supporting as they are well-branched and twiggy. They are also pliable. Smooth willow is best for bending as an edging round long grass or edging a border and it comes in satisfying earthy colours. You can buy both willow and hazel. Birch is also useful for staking plants because it is twiggy and pliable.

If you have a large enough garden, four or five mature hazel bushes (planted in a quiet corner) will provide you with a sustainable supply of sticks. Coppice one bush during winter every second year in rotation. Coppicers work on a 7–10-year rotation which you can mimic by coppicing one bush every other year. Cut back every stem hard to leave stumps, then store the wood upright. It must be leafless when cut. The hazel litter from the bushes is an excellent medium for woodland plants. Hellebores and snowdrops love this environment.

Did you know? Most of our native trees do not die after they are cut down: the stump sends up a multitude of small, fast-growing stems which will eventually form new timber ('poles') that can be harvested after a decade or so. If a tree is repeatedly felled every decade it will develop a permanent base – the 'stool' – which can live indefinitely, increasing its girth slightly with every passing year. Some coppiced stools are 6m (20ft) wide. They are truly ancient – thousands of years old.

Organic Tip ✔

The life of stakes can be extended by years if you shave off the bark and outermost layer of sapwood (where all the nutrients are) from the part of the stake that goes in the ground. The tool to use is an old-fashioned draw knife.

SECRETS OF SUCCESS WITH STAKING

- Staking plants (according to the late Christopher Lloyd) is an art and not a chore, and it makes a huge difference to a border. If it's done well the supports don't show at all (see below).
- Staking should be done when the plant is two-thirds grown. It is often done in late April and May, but it will depend. Doing it then allows you to judge the width of the plant.
- Cut the thick bottom end of the stake or pea stick at a sharp angle so that it is easier to get into the ground.
- Push it in well and then surround the plant with a ring of stakes spaced about 20–30cm (8–12in) apart. Weave the twiggy tops together with string by going under and over to form a network of overhead stems just above the foliage. As the plant grows up it will poke through the gaps, hiding the twiggy cage.

5 Get Ready for Sowing and Planting

(*late January*)

THE SUN is gaining strength and the greenhouse can be a pleasant place to wash trays and pots ready for seed sowing. (A radio helps too.) This is a vital task. Cleanliness helps to prevent fungal attack, something that could see off your seedlings. So wash any pots you need for sowing. Round pots are better for seeds than square ones, which tend to hold water in the corners. The gaps between round pots also help ventilation. Always leave a gap of 1cm (½in) between the top of the pot and the top of the compost when filling pots. This allows water to drain away without washing the seeds over the edge.

Most gardeners use solid plastic seed trays or the thinner more disposable ones. These are saved from year to year and now is the time to brush off the debris and wash or wipe them down. Gloves and a bowl are vital equipment. If you're buying in the future, avoid trays with deep indentations in the base and overhanging lips. Both are hiding places for slugs and snails, as I discovered when I tripped up carrying one. I lost the seedlings and compost but several slugs in the grooves at the bottom clung on. I have never used one since.

Buy your compost now and, if you do a lot of seed sowing, invest in John Innes seed-sowing compost or another good compost recommended for sowing. This will be friable and fine and have a tiny bit of food. Too much food hampers seedling growth.

Did you know? John Innes is not a commercial brand. It is a recipe that was developed by the John Innes Centre in 1933 following problems with the germination of *Primula sinensis* seeds. The John Innes Centre has never produced the composts commercially or benefited financially from their production; it just supplied the recipe. John Innes contains seven parts loam, three parts peat and two parts sand, so it drains well and yet retains moisture. It can be rehydrated easily after drying out and the nutrients are delivered slowly.

Organic Tip ✔

Try to buy organic natural fertilizers like blood, fish and bone or chicken-manure products rather than synthetic fertilizers. The latter take lots of energy to produce and are rich in soluble nitrogen, which leaches out easily and gets into watercourses.

SECRETS OF SUCCESS – CHOOSING COMPOST WISELY

- Seed-sowing compost is designed for the job. Multipurpose isn't.
- John Innes No. 1 is ideal for pricking out and potting on rooted cuttings.
- John Innes No. 2 contains double the amount of nutrients in No. 1. It's for house plants and vegetable plants in medium-sized pots.
- John Innes No. 3 has the most nutrients of all. It's perfect for greedy plants like tomatoes and for large pots containing shrubs and trees.
- Loam contains essential micro-nutrients and some organic matter which provides a slow release of nitrogen to the plant.
- Sphagnum moss peat increases the total porosity and improves aeration and water retention. Peat decomposes slowly into humus. It is being phased out because extraction harms the environment.
- Coarse sand or grit allows excess water to drain from the compost, preventing waterlogging.

6 Greenhouse Care

(late January)

LIGHT levels are building up well, but in the greenhouse dirty glass can exclude lots of light just when you need it most. A hose and a car-wash tool will soon have your glass sparkling and (if your greenhouse is wooden) this is a good month to spruce up the paintwork with a coating of preservative. Most of us shy away from red cedar paint, which looks so brash, but there are plenty of easy-to-apply preservatives available now. Your garden seats and tables could probably do with a coating too.

I don't use strong chemicals inside my greenhouse. I rely on brushing it down and washing it with water. But do unplug any heaters etc., first. My tidying regime is thorough but not total. I don't usually brush away any clusters of eggs. They are often much-needed predators, like spiders. If you spot any yellow rockwool-like clusters, these belong to (*Cotesia glomerata*), an important predator of the Cabbage White butterfly, so they should be left *in situ*.

Many plants have been overwintering and by February they will be starting to grow again. Go through them and remove old or dead foliage. Tug them well by their stems. Vine weevil may have nibbled into their stems and roots. If you do find any damage, throw the plant away or move it somewhere far away. There will be casualties – dead sticks in pots – but you may want to leave those in case they snap into growth once it warms up.

Did you know? The discovery of a giant waterlily in the River Amazon in the nineteenth century revolutionized greenhouse design. The waterlily provoked strong competition among the British aristocracy to see who could get a cutting to flower first. The Duke of Devonshire's gardener, Sir Joseph Paxton, was the winner, in November 1849. The Duke presented Queen Victoria with one of the first flowers and named it *Victoria amazonica* in her honour. This lily had huge leaves with ribbed veining underneath, which Paxton described as 'transverse girders and supports', making them strong enough to carry the weight of his daughter, Annie. Inspired, Paxton developed a greenhouse design which formed the basis for the Crystal Palace, a building four times the size of St Peter's in Rome.

Organic Tip ✔

Polystyrene fish boxes make excellent containers for starting off dahlias as they keep plants warm at the root. Try to make drainage holes with a skewer if you can.

SECRETS OF SUCCESS

- Aluminium greenhouses cool down more quickly in winter than wooden ones, and also heat up much faster in summer – so generally wooden greenhouses provide more ambient and even temperatures.
- Heated greenhouses are a luxury. Generally an unheated greenhouse with a frost-breaking electric heater is fine. If there's no electricity, fleece your plants in winter.
- Get a maximum–minimum thermometer and hang it up, and then you will be able to judge extremes – the coldest and hottest temperatures every day.
- Greenhouses in shady positions are difficult to use after April when leaves overhead open out.
- Opinions vary about how to line up your greenhouse: an east–west ridge gets a more even light, but north–south works well too. Accessibilty is the main thing. Can you get to it and can you get a hose to it?

FEBRUARY

February is an exciting month for the gardener because flowers appear at ground level and every year they seem to arrive in a slightly different order. If it's a sunny year the cyclamen and crocus may appear first, even when the temperatures are cold. If it's warm and grey, it may be the snowdrop that braves the weather first. It doesn't matter to most of us who wins the 'race of the year' to be the first to flower. It's the fact that the garden is coming back to life that cheers the gardener's soul.

The temperatures may be warm enough to produce a waft of fragrance and there are many winter-flowering plants that try to lure in a pollinator in this way. Often these fragrant flowers are surprisingly tiny and insignificant, but winter is a season full of subtleties.

1 Line Up Some Winter Fragrance

(early February)

GARDEN centres should be well stocked with plants by February and some of those will be fragrant shrubs. These can be positively spirit-boosting in the lull between winter and spring. As Beverley Nichols (1898–1983) wrote, 'To be overcome by the fragrance of flowers is a delectable form of defeat.'

The sarcococcas are the finest scented winter shrubs for container use and their common name, sweet box, sums them up well, for this compact Asian evergreen has box-like foliage. The most elegant form of all, *Sarcococca confusa*, has small green leaves and ivory flowers. These flowers are clusters of pendent stamens, yet they pack a powerful lily-like scent that travels over a wide area. *S. hookeriana* has pink stamens and often the foliage looks olive-green and less pristine, although I think the flowers are even more heavily scented than those of *S. confusa*.

Seek them out in garden centres and place one (or more) close to your door, either as single specimens or among ivies and small bulbs. A sarcococca can stay in the same container for a year or two, but release it into the garden after that.

SECRET OF SUCCESS

- Place winter-fragrant plants close to a gate or doorway that gets afternoon sunshine. Then the flowers will benefit from the warmth of the early afternoon before temperatures begin falling again. This encourages maximum scent.

Did you know? Once unknown in British gardens, sarcococcas became popular in the mid-1990s following collections from Yunnan in China by the Royal Botanic Gardens at Kew. *S. confusa* was said to have been given its name because it was recorded in the wild, probably in the late nineteenth century by the botanist Augustine Henry, who sent the black berries to Britain, but when another collector (probably Ernest 'Chinese' Wilson) followed in Henry's footsteps he could not locate it. It has never been found in the wild since and may have been a one-off hybrid.

EARLY-FLOWERING SCENTED SHRUBS

Azara microphylla
A tall, leggy shrub that produces small, almost invisible yellow stars in February. It oozes vanilla fragrance.

***Daphne bholua* 'Jacqueline Postill'**
The only truly evergreen January-flowering daphne. Columnar, with shiny oval green leaves and waxy lilac-mauve flowers with a heavenly scent.

***Skimmia* x *confusa* 'Kew Green'**
Small evergreen with lilac-like heads of ivory-white, lightly scented flowers in spring. The tight, pale-green buds provide interest between autumn and early spring. Good in containers.

***Chimonanthus praecox* (Wintersweet)**
A large shrub producing translucent flowers on bare stems in late winter. Strongly scented and a lovely plant to cut for indoor use. Needs a warm position but is untidy in summer.

***Mahonia* x *media* 'Winter Sun'**
Prickly leaves with long, slender racemes of pale-yellow flowers that arch upwards and outwards from November through to February. Subtle lily-of-the-valley scent. This mahonia will flower in shade.

***Viburnum* x *bodnantense* 'Dawn'**
This long-flowering shrub produces masses of rich-pink flowers from November to March. Frost browns them, however. A tall shrub for a boundary edge. Intense hyacinth scent in November.

Organic Tip ✔

Winter containers of flowering shrubs provide a rich nectar source for the earliest bees. Rest winter containers in the summer months by putting them in quiet shade. Feed and water them well up until late August, then allow the foliage to toughen up.

2 Cut Back Winter Jasmine

(*early February*)

WINTER jasmine (*Jasminum nudiflorum*) obligingly flowers in winter, often beginning in November and carrying on in flurries. It flowers on new wood and responds well to being cut back now or straight after flowering. A pair of shears does the job well – it isn't a precision task for secateurs. An annual skinhead haircut encourages lots of twiggy new growth and these shiny olive-green stems show off the bright-yellow flowers to perfection. It's one plant that every garden should contain because those yellow stars are invaluable winter warmers whether picked for the house or left in the garden.

This versatile shrub, which seems to grow in any soil and situation, can be clipped round doorways and windows, or it can be shaped to form a hedge or an arch. However, just like a poodle, it must be clipped and not allowed to straggle untidily. The warmer the position, the earlier the flowers. It's one of the few flowers capable of gracing November and it never seems to brown in winter frost. The flowers seem to open only in clement spells, so it comes and goes through winter. It doesn't have a scent, but then you can't have everything!

Did you know? *J. nudiflorum* was collected by Robert Fortune in 1843 on a 3-year trip to China, where it had been cultivated for centuries.

In 1848 and 1853 Fortune returned to China to collect tea plants for the East India Company with the aim of ending the Chinese monopoly on tea production. His plants and seedlings were transported to India in sealed glass boxes called Wardian cases with mixed success. However, it was partly due to Fortune's efforts that India became a tea-growing country.

Organic Tip ✔

When planting a new winter jasmine, lay it on its side in a long trench and bury the stems. Then it should shoot all the way along its length. You can also do this with clematis and honeysuckle, and this establishes the plant faster than planting it straight into the soil.

SECRET OF SUCCESS

- If you want November flowers, choose a south-facing position and clip before birds take up residence. They love to nest in twiggy winter jasmines grown on walls.

3 Cut Down Grasses

(mid-February)

THE NATURALISTIC planting style – championed by the Dutch garden designer Piet Oudolf and widely adopted – makes use of tall grasses and perennials, which tend to flower late before fading beautifully into winter. They provide contours and silhouettes in low light and catch the frost to perfection. However, now that spring is on the horizon (and hopefully the hardest weather is behind us), it's a good time to cut down these plants. Arm yourself with goggles and gloves, as some of the grasses are brutal, and wear thick sleeves. By now any remaining stems will be very woody.

Some tall grasses, including varieties of *Miscanthus sinensis*, shoot inside the old stems early on. Cut them back with one-handed shears (these look like large scissors) or secateurs. Also cut perennials down, but don't disturb any plants. It is too early to move or divide things. However, if you feel work needs to be done, make a note of what to do later.

The material you are cutting away is quite woody and tough so you could shred it mechanically. Failing that, cut it into sections as you add it to the compost heap. Tidy and weed as you go.

Miscanthus, calamagrostis, panicum and molinia can all be cut back now because they are very hardy. However, pennisetums and stipas are less robust and are best left intact until mid-April. Then they can be given a tidy rather than a severe cutting back.

Pampas grass (*Cortaderia*) is evergreen, but the foliage can be carefully tweaked and tidied now. Do take care: the edges of the leaves are razor sharp. Other evergreen plants (like *Kniphofia*) can also be carefully tidied, but these are never cut back hard.

Did you know? Although the naturalistic style is always attributed to the Dutch, it actually began in Germany with plant breeders like Karl Foerster (1874–1970), Ernst Pagels (1913–2007) and George Arends (1862–1952). Foerster, who was more landscape architect than nurseryman, wanted to create natural-looking vistas suited to northern Europe and pioneered the use of grasses, or 'nature's hair' as he called them.

VARIETIES OF GRASSES AND PERENNIALS

***Miscanthus sinensis* 'Ferner Osten'**
Moody-red heads fade to mink-brown. 1.5m (5ft) or more.

***Eupatorium maculatum* 'Riesenschirm' AGM**
Stiff, dark stems of whorled leaves topped by fluffy 20cm (8in) wide heads of moody purple–pink flowers which attract the butterflies and pick up the colour of grasses and flowers containing pink or purple tones. 1.8m (6ft).

***Echinacea purpurea* 'Fatal Attraction'**
Echinaceas provide the wow factor, flowering from July until autumn, before forming a stiff, black-centred seed head. 'Fatal Attraction' has bright pink flowers with broad middles held on thick, dark stems. 60–90cm (2–3ft).

***Veronicastrum virginicum* 'Lavendelturm'**
Whorled foliage topped by tapering, upright lavender-blue flowers. 1.5m (5ft).

***Rudbeckia fulgida* var. *sullivantii* 'Goldsturm' AGM**
Dark-brown button middles framed by a neat ring of yellow petals. A good clump will support 100 blooms. 90cm (3ft).

***Monarda* 'Scorpion' (bergamot)**
Lovers of damper soil, these stiff-stemmed plants have pinkish flowers that emerge from a pepperpot head. The violet-purple 'Scorpion' flowers later (and for longer) and the bracts supporting the flowers are a deep sooty purple. 1.2m (4ft).

***Sanguisorba officinalis* 'Red Thunder'**
The bobble-headed, tall forms of this plant almost look like grasses when seen in profile and several from Asia flower usefully late here. 'Red Thunder' (collected in Korea) will reach 1.5m (5ft), producing wine-red bobbles from August onwards.

***Aconitum* x *carmichaelii* 'Arendsii' AGM**
Rich blues glow like evening stars in the late border and this thick-stemmed aconitum has deep-blue flowers and green glossy foliage. 1.8m (6ft).

SECRETS OF SUCCESS FOR NATURALISTIC PLANTING

- If planting tall grasses, opt for equally tall perennials so that you get a proper swathe.
- Naturalistic borders rely on stiff-stemmed plants that don't need staking.
- These borders should be planted in open situations. This makes the plants sturdier and stiffer-stemmed. Then when frost descends the plants sparkle in winter sunlight.
- Select a few excellent perennials and grasses and plant in groups of three, five, seven or nine, depending on space. If you have room, planting in large swathes, allowing a square metre for each group of plants, is particularly pleasing, but create a ribbon rather than a block.

4 Prune Roses

(late February)

PRUNING keeps roses vigorous and healthy. Now is the best time to tackle it, while they are still dormant but likely to start into growth very soon. Different types of roses are pruned in different ways. As a general rule, old-fashioned roses and shrub roses are more lightly pruned and the main leaders are cut back by a third. Hybrid teas can be cut back hard to 10–15cm (4–6in). Floribundas should be left with stems between 30cm and 45cm (12in and 18in) in length. Always aim to create an open structure. Some gardeners remove one old branch from the base every year, but this depends on the shape of the rose.

Many rambling roses produce vigorous leaders from the base every summer and these are generally tied in when pliable (see page 164) before winter takes hold.

Climbing roses vary in habit and vigour, but they should all be hard-pruned when they are planted to encourage a strong framework.

Tie in the new shoots produced in the first year, tugging them downwards to defy gravity. This will ensure your climber flowers all over from tip to toe. Climbers and ramblers on a pergola should have their stems coiled round and looped downwards when they reach the top. These techniques slow the sap, preventing leggy growth and causing more flower buds to develop. Always check ties and supports now too.

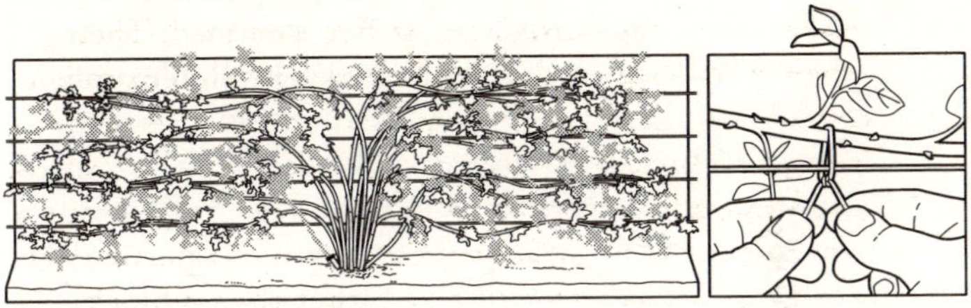

Repeat-flowering roses are often more popular than 'once-and-only' roses which flower just once in June. However, repeat-flowerers ration out their flowers rather meagrely, whereas once-and-onlies drip with flowers magnificently for 3 weeks. These are the roses that make June special. The gallicas, almost all ramblers and some old-fashioned roses are once-and-onlies.

Did you know? The China rose laid the foundation of modern repeat-flowering roses. The first specimens were brought back to Europe by the Dutch East India Company with consignments of tea in the late eighteenth century. (See also page 97).

Organic Tip ✔

If your roses develop aphids, please don't spray (even with soapy water) because predatory insects and birds will soon home in on them and will be poisoned. If the aphids really offend you, put on your gardening gloves and squeeze them with your fingers.

SECRETS OF SUCCESS

- Always use sharp secateurs and wear thick gloves. Have a pruning saw ready too.
- Study each plant carefully before pruning.
- Start by removing any dead, dying or diseased wood – the 3 Ds.
- Remove any crossing branches.
- When you have decided where to cut, make your cuts 5 mm (¼in) above an outward-facing bud. The new growth will then develop on the outer edges of the bush, allowing the bush to keep an open shape.
- Slant cuts downwards away from the buds. This encourages rain to drain away from the buds.
- If you see dark marks inside the rose stem after pruning, you need to cut lower until you reach completely white wood.

ROSE VARIETIES

'Champagne Moment'
My favourite bomb-proof Kordes floribunda, with healthy foliage and clusters of creamy pale-apricot flowers.

'Warm Wishes'
Award-winning, medium-sized rose with well-spaced clusters of peach–coral flowers enhanced by dark foliage. Very free-flowering and continuous.

'Madame Alfred Carrière'
Healthy, vigorous, ivory-white climbing rose capable of flowering in shade. Always flowers late. Almost thornless stems make it a perfect pergola rose.

'New Dawn'
Silver-pink, repeat-flowering rambler. Healthy olive-green foliage and lots of modern-looking pink roses.

'Bonica'
A low-growing pink rose that repeat-flowers, even in poor soil. Packed with flowers.

5 Sow Sweet Peas

(late February)

SWEET PEAS (*Lathyrus odoratus*) are the perfect cut-and-come-again flower and late February is an excellent time to sow them, especially in colder areas. Real enthusiasts sow seeds in autumn and overwinter them, but this can be difficult and you will still get excellent results from sowing now.

Use deep pots, up to 22cm (9in) in depth, or toilet-roll centres packed into a seed tray – one or two seeds per tube. Almost fill the pots or rolls with John Innes No. 1. Place the seeds and lightly cover them with a thin layer of compost before putting them on a windowsill or in a greenhouse. The ideal germination temperature is 15°C (59°F). However, once the seeds germinate move them somewhere cooler, where it's ideally only 8–10°C (46.5–50°F). A cold frame is ideal – but always protect the seedlings from mice. They consume sweet pea plants and seeds whenever they get the chance.

Once the seedlings have three pairs of true leaves, pinch out the tops to encourage bushier plants. Then, when April comes, harden them off outside for a week before planting them into fertile soil. Space them 15cm (6in) apart and support them with wigwams made from canes and string, or with twiggy supports. Never let the seedlings dry out, and feed them weekly with a potash-rich tomato food once flowering begins.

Organic Tip ✔

Pollen beetles adore sweet pea flowers but they don't do any harm. If you pick your sweet peas and leave them outside in water in a cool place, the pollen beetles disappear.

Did you know? Henry Eckford (1823–1905) of Wem in Shropshire perfected the grandiflora strain of sweet peas and Wem still holds an sweet pea show every July in his honour. In 1901 Silas Cole, head gardener to Earl Spencer, found a large sweet pea with much frillier flowers sporting from a popular Eckford variety called 'Prima Donna'. He then bred a bright pink, huge and luscious sweet pea and saved five seeds, but lost three to mice. Eventually Silas Cole exhibited 'Countess Spencer' at the National Sweet Pea Society's first show at the Royal Aquarium in London in 1901. It was a significant breakthrough at the time because 'Spencer' sweet peas have much larger flowers and an excellent scent.

SECRETS OF SUCCESS

- Choose named varieties rather than mixtures, as seed quality is often better and you can blend your own colour schemes.
- Grow under cover and then harden off for a week.
- Transplant into fertile, well-drained soil in a sunny situation.
- Add your supports and then water thoroughly straight after planting. However, do not water during the hottest part of the day.
- Once the first flowers appear, water with a potash-rich food like comfrey tea (see page 103) or branded tomato food.
- Pick every other day and always remove any pods.
- Allow the plant to set seed in August if you want to collect seeds. Sweet peas cannot be cross-pollinated and their seeds will always come true.

VARIETIES OF SWEET PEA

'Gwendoline'
Large, wavy pink blooms suffused with white. A strong performer and heavily scented.

'Mrs Collier'
A creamy-white grandiflora with a heavenly scent.

'Charlie's Angel'
Large, fragrant silver-blue flowers tinted with lavender.

'Our Harry'
A clear-blue – the most reliable true blue of all.

6 Edging Borders and Lawn Care

(late February)

AT THIS time of year the gullies and edges between the border and the lawn need to be thoroughly tidied and neatly edged in order to give your garden a pristine, well-cared-for look. If the edges are not very straight, use a line (a length of string held tautly between two sticks will do) to get a completely straight edge. If they're curved, you can lay out a hosepipe to get a gentle curve, then follow that line. Angle a half-moon edger (a necessity for all gardeners) slightly away from your body, rather than straight down. This exaggerates the edge, making it look deeper, and it aids drainage. It also prevents weed seedlings from germinating in the tight groove at the bottom where the lawn edge meets the soil.

Once a smart edge is achieved, take the time to trim it with long edging shears after mowing. This makes a huge difference to a border. Weed thoroughly, taking care to eradicate all dandelions before they flower. Rake the grass thoroughly. Spike the lawn to aerate it and stimulate soil organisms and root growth, and apply lawn sand to improve drainage if necessary.

As March approaches it will be time to make the first cut, but do wait for the grass to begin to grow. The first cut should merely 'top' the grass and tidy it. Close-cutting at this stage could result in severe yellowing or browning. Two gentle cuts are generally sufficient this month.

However, by April the mowing regime will be well under way. Mow often enough to stop grass growing away. Dig out patches of coarse grass or pernicious weeds and re-seed bare patches.

Organic Tip ✔

More man-made chemicals are bought to treat lawns than anything else. These include mosskillers, wormkillers, antkillers and weedkillers. Many are expensive to produce, and many are harmful to the environment. Garden-users come into contact with their lawn constantly – so perhaps it's more sensible to rake out the moss and weed out the dandelions than attack them chemically.

SECRETS OF SUCCESS

- A spring-tine rake can be used to scarify grass. Pull it through the grass and it will remove all the dead thatch, allowing the rain to get to the roots and drain away.
- A twice-yearly application of lawn food helps. Apply in early March and again in September. Mow the lawn at the normal height, then spread the fertilizer at the required rate. However, if you want wild flowers in your lawn do not add fertilizer.
- Always apply lawn food on a still day just before rain. Try to avoid using the lawn for 2 or 3 days after application.
- Mow 3 days after feeding.

Did you know? Motor mowers were not commonly available until the 1890s when lightweight petrol engines and small steam-powered units became available.

VARIETIES OF GRASS IN LAWN MIXTURES

Perennial Rye Grass (*Lolium perenne*)
Rye grass is tough and durable and it is found in many mixtures. It germinates within 10 days and forms a dense lawn. It dislikes shade and isn't drought-tolerant, but quickly bounces back after rain.

Fescue (*Festuca* species)
Several different fescues can be included in lawn mixtures. These fine-leaved grasses thrive in well-drained soil in the wild and form the basis of fine lawn mixtures, but to a lesser degree they are also contained in family lawn mixtures. They are slow-growing and tend to stay green in dry weather.

Browntop Bent (*Agrostis tenuis*)
This fine green grass is added to mixtures designed to thrive in shady areas.

Smooth-stalked Meadow Grass (*Poa pratensis*)
Another grass for shade, with drought tolerance. This grey-green grass may take 21 days to come up.

MARCH

Most gardens should be coming back to life after the long winter sleep and on certain clement days when the temperature rises there's a hint of summer in the air. Blossom is tantalizingly close to opening, the earliest spring bulbs are out and leafy buds are plumping up, ready to burst on tree and hedge.

The temptation is to rush out and plant and sow, but (as the soothsayer so famously said to Julius Caesar) 'Beware the Ides of March.' We are still hovering between winter and spring. However, there are jobs that can be done and sheltered parts of the garden under deciduous trees should be looking their best in early spring. The rest will soon catch up.

1 Plant an Early-spring Container

(early March)

RAID YOUR garden centre or local nursery now and create some instant spring colour close to a doorway – the shelves will be groaning under the weight of all those spring-flowering plants.

First seek out some good foliage for your backbone planting, choosing only plants that are at the peak of perfection. Mix the leafy textures and try to find hardy ferns, green-leaved ivies, grasses, evergreen shrubs and shawl-like heuchera foliage. Stick to a colour theme. Concentrate on all-green, or shades of gold and green, or cream and green. Silvers are too summery in March. Your choice may depend on what's available, so go with an open mind.

If you decide on all-green foliage, white flowers will look pristinely elegant. White pansies, crocus 'Jeanne d'Arc', snowdrops and Christmas roses should all be on offer and can be used in your garden afterwards. If your foliage is splashed in gold, bring it to life with yellow flowers mingled among blue- and purple-flowering bulbs. This is a vibrant combination that creates its own sunshine, so it could light up a dull corner. White and cream foliage is cooler in tone: adding pink heather, plummy hellebores or purple-flowering bulbs will create clean sparkle.

March will allow you a wider use of materials and you could adopt a wicker basket, a wooden trug or a galvanized container for your display. Try to use one grass for vertical accent and at least one trailing plant (like an ivy) to extend the arrangement and link it to the ground.

Did you know? The Romans used terracotta pots to propagate their plants, bending and pegging shoots down into them (or rooting layered plants). Cato, in *De Agri Cultura* (169 BC), explains how, when the plant had outgrown the pot, the pots were cracked so that the roots could penetrate the soil. The Greek philosopher Theophrastus (371–286 BC) also describes large terracotta pots being used for cedars and palms in Persia during the fourth century BC.

SECRETS OF SUCCESS

- Stand your container on pot feet if at all possible so that water can drain away more freely. This is a necessity for all pots that stand outside in winter, but it will also help throughout the year.
- When choosing plants, try to identify the star plant of your group (a showy one) and put that in first, not dead centre but to one side. Then infill, planting densely.
- Once the backbone foliage is in place, put a small empty pot at the forefront of the container. You can use this to ring the changes every 10 days or so by dropping another small pot of flowering bulbs etc., inside the permanent one.
- Your plants should not dwarf the container. As a rule of thumb, aim for between a quarter and a half in extra height – i.e., if your pot is 60cm (2ft) tall, your plants could reach up to 30cm (12in) more, although this will depend on the shape of the pot. Too much height will make pots unsteady.
- Break the monotony and add a 'firework' plant – perhaps the spiky green and golden sedge *Carex oshimensis* 'Evergold'.

Organic Tip ✔

Containers are easier to manage if plants are put into loam-based compost (like John Innes), because this not only retains moisture better but also delivers the plant food more slowly and steadily. Use slow-release pelleted plant food in containers designed for long-term use.

WINNING COMBINATIONS

Orange violas smoulder against smoke-brown carex studded with a small purple crocus like 'Tricolor'.

Punctuate pink heathers with frosty-leaved lamiums, pulmonarias and marbled-leaved spring-flowering cyclamen.

Primroses abound now, and the postbox reds lift rich evergreen foliage, or glow dramatically against the black strappy grass-like *Ophiopogon planiscapus* 'Nigrescens'.

Pale-pink flowers shimmer against plummy or red-veined silver heucheras.

2 Sow Hardy Annuals

(early March)

EARLY MARCH is a good time to sow hardy annuals. However, half-hardy annuals (including zinnias, African marigolds and nicotiana) should not be sown until mid-April at the earliest. Check the details on the seed packets, looking carefully for the words 'hardy annual' (HA) or 'half-hardy annual' (HHA).

Use full-sized seed trays and seed-sowing compost. Fill to within 5cm (¼in) from the top. Water well, using tapwater that has been allowed to stand in a can. This allows the water to warm up and the chlorine in treated mains water to evaporate. Lightly sprinkle the seeds over the surface and cover lightly with compost.

Seeds should germinate within 7–14 days. You can sow cosmos, cornflower, clary and annual scabious in this way – see Hardy Annuals opposite. However, pot marigold (*Calendula officinalis*) seeds are large enough to handle and can be sown directly on to the ground should you wish, but wait until mid-April.

Once the seedlings have reached 5–7.5cm (2–3in) in height you can tackle them in two ways. You can prick them out individually into small, round plastic pots and grow them on until the roots fill the pot. Alternatively, you can let the seedlings reach 10–15cm (4–6in) and then tear off a small cluster of three to five to plant straight into the ground. If you adopt the latter method, keep the seedlings watered after planting.

Did you know? Annuals are the most attractive flowers of all to bees and hoverflies because they ooze nectar. These highly desirable insects pollinate your plants and hoverflies have predatory larvae that devour aphids, whitefly and other pests.

Organic Tip ✔

Poppy seeds are very fine and difficult to see and are best sown a few at a time into modular trays, 6 × 4in (15 × 10cm) size. The seeds form a poppy plug that can then be planted outside. Ladybird poppies, Papaver commutatum, *are a great addition.*

SECRETS OF SUCCESS

- Use mains water, not water-butt water. The latter will encourage fungal disease.
- Use warmed water delivered by a can with a fine rose. Drenching seeds this early in the year will lead to failure.
- Harden off seedlings before planting out. Stand them on a table outside.
- Make regular slug checks at dusk. Remember slugs come out at night to seek their prey.
- Dead-heading keeps annuals in flower for much longer.
- Towards the end of their life, allow them to set seed. Collect seeds on dry days at midday.

HARDY ANNUALS

***Cosmos bipinnatus* (Cosmos)**
A feathery-leaved Mexican daisy in pretty shades of pink and white. Cosmos keeps going until late autumn, so it is highly desirable. Many types on offer.

***Calendula officinalis* (Pot Marigold)**
An orange daisy with edible petals. Lots of variety, but my all-time favourite is the mahogany-eyed 'Indian Prince'.

***Centaurea cyanus* (Blue Cornflower)**
A willowy plant that, if dead-headed, will flower for months. The preferred annual of the red-tailed bumble bee (*Bombus lapidarius*).

***Salvia horminium* (Clary Sage)**
Colourful bracts (in white, pink or deep-blue) make this an everlasting pleasure for gardeners and bees. Easy and long-performing.

***Scabiosa atropurpurea* (Annual Scabious)**
These come in dark, almost black shades (as in 'Chile Black'), sorbet shades (as in 'Beaujolais Bonnets') and clear white.

3 Plant Alpines for Early-spring Colour

(mid-March)

ALPINE PLANTS are usually confined to pots, troughs or alpine screes in an attempt to emulate their high-altitude positions on well-drained mountain slopes. They reward the gardener with early flowers, and this is the best month to enjoy many of them and to go out and buy them. Neatly formed and diminutive, they flower in the open when little else does. Some are so demanding and difficult that they need an alpine house with open sides to keep them dry in winter. Others are easier: they can be managed outside as long as there is excellent drainage. These are the ones that garden centres stock.

In the wild, most are kept dry in winter by snow cover and cold weather acts as a desiccant. The snow melts slowly and the water drains away sharply due to the steep terrain. As a result, alpines never sit in water; it revives them just enough for them to flower. However, easier alpine plants found naturally on flatter terrain will grow happily on a well-drained, sloping scree constructed of grit, stone and boulders. Most prefer alkaline to neutral conditions, although there are some that thrive only on acid soil. Alpines mix well with diminutive bulbs like crocus and species tulips, and together they make early spring a more colourful affair.

Did you know? Rockeries were a Victorian obsession and one landscape gardener, James Pulham (1820–98), invented his own recipe for making an artificial rock called Pulhamite. He used it to cement natural rocks together and to form boulders between natural outcrops. Every grand-house owner aspired to a Pulhamite rockery. When he died he took the closely guarded recipe with him to the grave.

CREATING A SCREE

- Prepare the site by removing all perennial weeds.
- Arrange the larger rocks and cobbles, and try to create a slope to aid drainage.
- Cover the area with a 50:50 soil and grit mixture and top-dress with coarse grit or pea gravel. Replace regularly.
- Don't add any fertilizer. Alpines enjoy poor soil.
- Plant your alpines by raking back the gravel and placing the gritty mixture you remove in a bucket. Put your plant in and rake the gravel round the plant. A narrow trowel is the most useful tool here.
- Buy your alpines between March and August to ensure that you have an array of plants flowering in different months.

EASY ALPINES

Androsace sempervivoides **AGM**
Tight mats of shiny green leaves. Bright-pink flowers in March–April. 5cm (2in).

Dianthus alpinus **'Joan's Blood' AGM**
Small, deep-red single flowers in May–June. 12cm (5in).

Phlox douglasii **'Boothman's Variety' AGM**
Dark-eyed, mauve-pink single flowers above narrow foliage in May–June. 10cm (4in).

Saxifraga **Southside Seedling Group AGM**
Sprays of white flowers attractively spotted in red above silvery rosettes in May–June. Good in a well-drained, slightly shady spot. 30cm (12in).

Campanula portenschlagiana **AGM**
Vigorous, spreading evergreen with masses of pale, lavender-blue bells between May and August. Needs space 15cm (6in).

Organic Tip ✔

Gravel chips and stones work well with alpines in several ways. They filter the water in winter, creating better drainage. They keep the roots cool in sunny weather and they also hold the heat and throw warmth upwards. The downside is that they encourage seedlings.

4 Cut Down Viticella Clematis

(*mid-March*)

ALTHOUGH it's a little too early to cut back penstemons and other tender plants, it is the perfect time to reduce summer-flowering viticella clematis to their lowest buds. These scrambling clematis flower from July until September on this year's wood, producing an abundance of smaller flowers up to 5cm (2in) in diameter. These viticellas (which are marked 'Vt.' in the *RHS Plant Finder*) are smothered in lots of flowers and this allows them to fit into the flower border effortlessly.

Viticella flowers vary in shape. Some are slightly twisted and asymmetrical with greenish 'petals'; others have nodding dark bells and resemble the true Spanish species *Clematis viticella*. There are also flat, open-flowered forms and double forms like the navy-blue 'Mary Rose' and the rose-purple 'Purpurea Plena Elegans'. Viticella means small vine, and these clematis should not be confused with earlier-flowering or highly bred large-flowered clematis that produce only one or two huge flowers. These large-flowered varieties are both trimmed back very lightly after flowering, but only if needed: cutting them back hard will kill them.

Every clematis sold has concise pruning instructions on the label, so keep the label somewhere safe so that you can look them up if in doubt. Viticella flowers come in a range of blue, purple, red-pink and white and they make ideal partners for once-and-only-flowering roses. Or you could allow them to scramble over shrubs, or climb a trellis.

Did you know? The double viticella clematis 'Purpurea Plena Elegans' was written about in 1629 but was lost to cultivation until the great plantsman Graham Stuart Thomas (1909–2003) rediscovered it growing at Abbotswood Garden near Stow-on-the-Wold in the 1960s. Nowadays its dusky plum-red pompoms grace many gardens.

SECRETS OF SUCCESS

- The best time to plant is in spring or early autumn.
- Water all new clematis very well in their first growing season. They are grown in compost that can dry out.
- When pruning in March, use sharp secateurs and go to the base of the plant, selecting the large buds about 30cm (12in) from the ground. Cut cleanly just above these, then remove the old stems.
- Don't plant viticellas next to spring-flowering alpina or macropetala clematis. These need only gentle tidying after flowering in April, and separating the inevitable tangle of mixed stems (if the two types are planted together) is an impossibility.
- All clematis (regardless of type) prefer moist but well-drained soil and a cool root run.

Organic Tip ✔

Viticella clematis are bred from a species found in southern Europe, particularly Spain. They tolerate drier conditions naturally and they never suffer from clematis wilt.

VARIETIES

'Étoile Violette' AGM
The best viticella and the earliest to flower, producing purple flowers with widely spaced tepals surrounding a light-golden boss of stamens.

'Betty Corning' AGM
This silver-mauve clematis produces masses of sweetly fragrant, bell-shaped flowers on long stems from mid-June onwards. Each consists of four slightly frilled tepals and the new flowers are smaller and darker before they open widely. An excellent clematis for covering a bare fence. In the distance it looks blue-grey rather than pinkish.

'Polish Spirit' AGM
A dark violet-purple clematis which is a useful companion for rambling roses. It begins flowering in mid-July, clothing the spent rose with flowers. The flowers, which often have four wide tepals, have a dark middle.

'Royal Velours' AGM
Less vigorous than most viticellas, but the velvet-textured flowers, more wine-red than purple, have overlapping tepals which form a round, compact flower in July–August.

'Alba Luxurians' AGM
One of the daintiest of the viticellas and not as vigorous as most. The first flowers can be completely green, but as the season wears on from July into August they become white with green tips. Each small, irregular flower has dark stamens and trembles on its long stem.

5 Start Off Dahlias

(late March)

IF YOU have a greenhouse it's time to start off dahlia tubers under glass. Check them over, making sure that they feel fleshy and firm. Using a general-purpose compost, partly fill individual large pots or deep trays. Wooden tomato trays are just the right depth for growing dahlias. Lay each tuber out so that the stem is above the compost. Add labels, then cover with compost and water well. Keep your tubers in the warmest place you have and new shoots will soon appear.

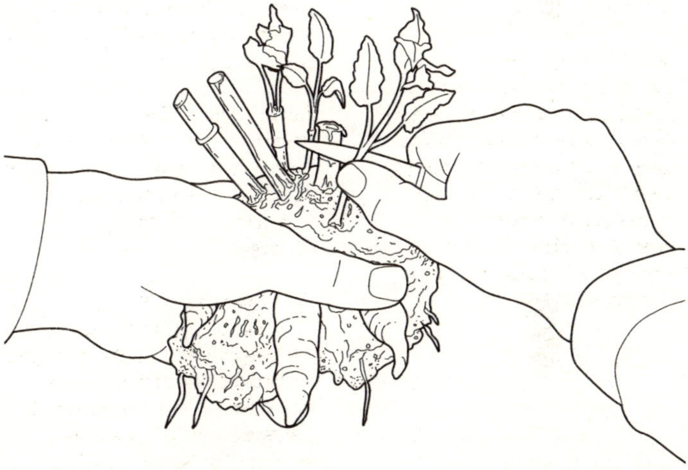

Cuttings can be taken from sprouting tubers when individual shoots measure 7.5cm (3in). Fill small round pots with John Innes No. 1 and, using a sharp knife, cut away the shoots just above where they join the crown. Trim the stem of the cutting below the joint under the lowest pair of leaves. Carefully remove the leaves too, leaving the top intact. Dampen the end of the prepared cutting, dip it in hormone rooting powder, place it in the compost and firm it in. Use one pot per variety to prevent confusion.

Cover your cuttings with a plastic bag, or put them in a propagator, and leave in a warm place out of direct sunlight. Rooted cuttings can be potted up into John Innes No. 2.

Organic Tip ✔

Slugs and snails can be a problem, especially with dark-leaved dahlias. Harden your plants off well for a week outside, then frisk them in the evenings to remove and destroy any gastropods having supper. Please do not use slug baits. Not only is the poison in them (metaldehyde) toxic to many life forms, but the copper they contain – used to colour the pellets blue – is particularly poisonous to toads, frogs and newts.

SECRETS OF SUCCESS

- Dahlias are frost-tender: the slightest hint of frost will check their growth and blacken their foliage. They must not be planted outside until the end of May at the earliest.
- Stake when you plant. Use three canes about 1m (3ft) in height, putting them in the ground in an equilateral triangle around the plant. Cap the canes with protective tops, then tie two separate lines of string round the canes, one higher than the other.
- Dead-head every few days and dahlias will flower non-stop. The pointed seed heads (which feel soggy to the touch) can look very similar to the bun-shaped buds when you're a novice, so get your eye in before you start.
- Water well in the first half of summer so that your plants establish. Feed with a potash-rich plant food, either home-made comfrey tea (see page 103) or liquid tomato feed.

Did you know? Some of the Mexican species (like *Dahlia imperialis*) are so tree-like in proportions that their hollow stems were used as irrigation pipes by the Aztecs. Their colloquial names were *cocoxchitl* and *acocotli*, literally meaning 'hollow pipe'.

VARIETIES

'David Howard'
A strong, easy dahlia with semi-double, butterscotch-orange flowers supported by dark, smouldering foliage. The perfect addition to an exotic, fiery border containing crocosmias, cannas and kniphofias. 1m (3ft).

'Bishop of Llandaff'
This 1920 vintage variety is probably still the best garden dahlia because it performs whatever the weather, producing an abundance of warm-red, peony-shaped blooms set against dark, divided foliage. 1m (3ft).

'Hillcrest Royal'
This dramatic purple, cactus-flowered dahlia has presence, and the strong-stemmed flowers seem to explode like fireworks as each sharply quilled petal radiates outwards. 1.3m (4ft).

'Magenta Star'
Clear-cut, bright-pink single flowers and dark foliage together with a pristinely neat habit make this new variety a show-stopper in the garden. The single flowers also attract butterflies and bees. 1m (3ft).

6 Dead-head Daffodils

(late March)

DEAD-HEAD daffodils to concentrate the bulbs' energy into producing next year's flowers. Remove the flower stalks at the base in formal settings. Or, if your daffodils are naturalized in grass, just snip the heads off. Water on a liquid plant food after dead-heading. Once you have dead-headed, allow the leaves to die back for at least 6 weeks. Do not attempt to tie the leaves together.

Large clumps can be split and redistributed as they fade. Those that aren't flowering may be 'blind' (not able to produce flowers) or the bulbs may be too small. Lifting the bulb will soon tell you. Small bulbs should be replanted, but big non-flowering ones could be discarded, or given a lighter, brighter position.

However, if you're trying to establish a wild colony (*Narcissus pseudonarcissus* subsp. *pseudonarcissus*) leave them to self-seed, as these species tend to spread in this way. A good wild-lookalike is 'W. P. Milner', an old variety from the nineteenth century with swept-forward, pale petals (20cm/8in). 'Topolino' is also excellent.

As a general rule, yellow daffodils flower in March and pale creams and whites (which are often scented) flower later. Taller varieties don't stand up to windy weather very well, so stick to good miniatures (or shorter varieties), ordering yellows, creams and whites to prolong the display.

Organic Tip ✔

It is now possible to buy bulbs of our native N. pseudonarcissus *subsp.* pseudonarcissus, *which looks very picturesque naturalized in grass.*

VARIETIES

'Jetfire' AGM
A 25cm (10in), bright-yellow daffodil, although technically not a miniature, that produces the brightest trumpet of all. It develops into bright orange and this jaunty variety naturalizes well.

'Rijnveld's Early Sensation' AGM
A taller, single-flowered, clear-yellow daffodil with a squat, flared trumpet. This early variety will flower in January if planted in early September. Divide regularly. 35cm (14in).

'W. P. Milner'
Wispy, pale-lemon flowers which mimic the wild daffodils of western England. The petals are swept forward to frame the elegant trumpet as demurely as the bonnet on a Jane Austen heroine. 20cm (8in).

'Topolino' AGM
An early trumpet daffodil with tasteful, two-tone yellow flowers. Pale outer petals surround a brighter, longer trumpet. 25cm (10in).

Did you know? Most taller daffodil varieties were bred for the cut-flower trade and the show bench. One cut-flower grower, Alec Gray of Camborne in Cornwall, stumbled on miniature varieties by accident when trying to breed earlier narcissi for the flower market. His most famous cultivar is 'Tête-à-Tête' (1949). 'Jumblie' (1952) and 'Quince' (1953) came from the same seed pod.

SECRETS OF SUCCESS

- All bulbous plants prefer good drainage.
- Plant narcissus bulbs in the first half of September to a depth of 10–15cm (4–6in). The bulbs shoot before Christmas, then lie in wait for warmer weather, with the growing tips hiding just below the surface of the ground until the weather warms up.
- Arrange them in informal groups of one variety, not in straight lines. Always avoid mixing varieties, as they will flower at different times. Later ones will be marred by fading seed pods.
- Later-flowering varieties are often scented and prefer a warmer position.
- Dead-head after flowering, if you wish. Don't be tempted to cut off or tie up your daffodil foliage. Allow the bulbs to die back naturally for at least 6 weeks, removing the leaves only once withered. You can mow the grass 6 weeks after the last one has flowered, however.
- Lift and divide congested, non-flowering clumps when they first appear in the early spring, or roughly 6 weeks after flowering.

APRIL

April brings a rush of blood to any gardener's head and it's a good thing too, for this is one of the most intensive months in the garden. Planting, sowing, dividing, potting, weeding and watering are all pressing matters and, if the evenings stay fine, a great deal can be achieved. A good month now will make the rest of the year so much easier.

The wild card is the weather. It can be wonderfully warm and, if it is, crack on. It can also be bitterly cold, and that means rain, sleet and snow stop play. In these frustrating conditions you may need to offer up a prayer to St Monica, the patron saint of patience.

1 Cut Down Dogwoods and Other Winter Stems

(early April)

DOGWOODS (*Cornus* species) shine in winter light when their waist-high stems catch the low sun, making a significant contribution to the winter garden. Some form twiggy shrubs; others produce pencil-thick stems that rise straight up from the ground. In each case it's only the young stems that are truly vivid. So now is the time to prune them and encourage a growth spurt so that they look pristine by next winter.

Some dogwoods produce thick, upright stems from creeping (or suckering) roots. They are best grown where space allows; they are not suitable for small gardens. Stems pop up some distance away from the original plant to form a loose screen, and stem colour can vary from olive-green to damson-black to bright-red (see overleaf). Their great strength is their ability to grow in water-logged, heavy soil and some of the best I've seen grow close to calm water. The mirrored effect adds another dimension visually, so if you have room close to a pond or lake these shrubs will add magic. The thicker-stemmed varieties need cutting back to ground level every April – a technique known as 'stooling'. They re-shoot quickly and provide plain-green, golden and variegated foliage. Many colour up well in autumn.

Twiggier dogwoods with flickering coral-pink stems are less resilient and are therefore treated more kindly. These include *C. sanguinea* 'Midwinter Fire'. Remove between half and a third of the old wood to encourage lots of flame-like growth. This lovely shrub also needs reasonable drainage.

SECRETS OF SUCCESS

- Always make sure that your shrubs have a couple of years to get going before you adopt this pruning regime.
- Once shrubs have been pruned, mulch to keep the soil moist and warm.
- When shaping any shrub or tree, think carefully before you cut anything away. Cut above outward-facing buds where appropriate. This will keep an open shape, allowing light and air into the tree.
- Plant where winter sun can light them up – perhaps among white-stemmed Himalayan birches.

WINTER STEM SHRUBS

***C. sericea* 'Flaviramea' AGM**
Upright, warm olive-green stems of pencil thickness.

***C. alba* 'Sibirica' AGM**
Upright, sealing-wax-red stems. A delight in winter.

***C. alba* 'Kesselringii'**
Upright, damson-black stems.

***C. sanguinea* 'Midwinter Fire'**
Twiggy shrub with flickering coral-pink and orange stems.

***Salix alba* var. *vitellina* 'Britzensis'**
Fine, marmalade-orange whips billow away from the trunk gracefully.

***Perovskia atriplicifolia* 'Blue Spire' AGM**
Needs a hot spot, but this Russian sage has a downy white 'tumbleweed' skeleton in winter.

***Rubus thibetanus* AGM**
One of the prickly ghost brambles with damson-bloomed, white arching stems.

Organic Tip ✔

Pruning cuts must be clean and sharp so that they heal cleanly and so prevent disease from entering the wood. Keen gardeners should acquire Felco tools suited to the job. Although expensive, with care these secateurs and loppers will outlast you.

Did you know? Dogwood is an old name that was recorded in the early seventeenth century. It is thought to have derived from the old West Country word 'dawk', meaning skewer. It was used to make skewers because the wood did not taint the meat. John Evelyn thought – wrongly – that the plant was called dogwood because it was not fit for any purpose. The black fruits are known as dogberries or houndberries.

2 Cut Back Penstemons and Mediterranean Plants

(early April)

PENSTEMONS are not terribly hardy due to their South American provenance, but now that spring has hopefully sprung, it's time to cut them back. Remove all the old stems to expose the new green shoots at the base. If some haven't started into growth yet they may be casualties of last winter. However, they are probably more likely to shoot into growth at the base if you cut them back now than if you leave them long and straggly. If they do fail, it's a great time to plant new ones.

Compost the old pieces of stem: they are not generally good for cutting material. Once cut back, your penstemons should grow away strongly and by June there will be plenty of shoots for cuttings (see page 80). Cuttings of favourite varieties should be taken every year, as penstemons are generally not long-lived or enduring.

These plants thrive in warm, sunny positions and always do best in warm, sunny summers. They enhance roses, peonies and all traditional herbaceous plants. Most importantly, they flower until very late into the year, providing spikes of flower to add those important vertical accents that every border needs.

Lots of other leggy plants can also be cut back now, including anthemis, santolinas, hardy sages, woody achilleas and rock roses (or helianthemums). Any perennial plant with damaged growth should also be tidied now and lots of dianthus (pinks) may well need a good haircut.

Did you know? Penstemon-breeding in Britain has been centred round Pershore in Worcestershire for almost 50 years. The 1960s Bird Series (including 'Raven', 'Osprey' and 'Blackbird') was bred there by a plum expert called Ron Sidwell. He chose his own garden, Bredon Springs, for its frost-free climate. A short distance away, Edward Wilson developed fifty Pensham varieties between 1980 and 2008. One named 'Ted's Purple' celebrates his achievement. Pershore College holds one of the Plant Heritage collections of penstemons.

Organic Tip ✔

Regular dead-heading is vital for penstemons, but in some varieties the dark seed heads look very similar to small buds. Look for the protruding cotton-like style that's left behind as the indicator of a spent flower.

SECRETS OF SUCCESS

- These plants need a warm, sunny position and a warm, sunny summer.
- Choose good varieties.
- Take cuttings regularly.
- Evict straggly old plants ruthlessly.
- Leave the top growth intact over winter.

VARIETIES

***Penstemon* 'Papal Purple'**
The longest-flowering penstemon I grow. Produces a succession of squat-tubed flowers from May until November on a compact plant.

***P. heterophyllus* 'Catherine de la Mare' AGM**
An early-flowering, sprawling penstemon covered in a forget-me-not mixture of blue- and pink-tinted flowers throughout summer and autumn.

***Penstemon* 'Andenken an Friedrich Hahn' AGM (also sold as 'Garnet')**
The best penstemon for hardiness, producing a continual supply of slender spikes of ruby–garnet-red flowers of a modest size.

***Penstemon* 'Stapleford Gem'**
A smoky silver-blue, like a cool opal, this smoulders in the border. Stately and taller than most.

***Penstemon* 'Pensham Plum Jerkum'**
Dusky damson-purple flowers etched in white. Poised and balanced, and shows off well in the border.

3 Divide and Propagate Perennials

(mid-April)

THIS IS the perfect time to think about dividing perennial plants, but only if they are looking congested or losing vigour. Don't be a slave to doing it every year. However, plants do look best planted in threes, fives, sevens or nines, so you may want to divide in order to make a better display. Avoid straight lines and blobs. Form a waving ribbon – with one plant spaced away from the others – for a natural effect.

Agapanthus, kniphofia (red hot pokers) and hemerocallis (day lilies) can only be divided in spring as losses occur if it is attempted in autumn. All three produce dense clumps that need sawing or cutting into chunky pieces, using a handsaw or a large kitchen knife.

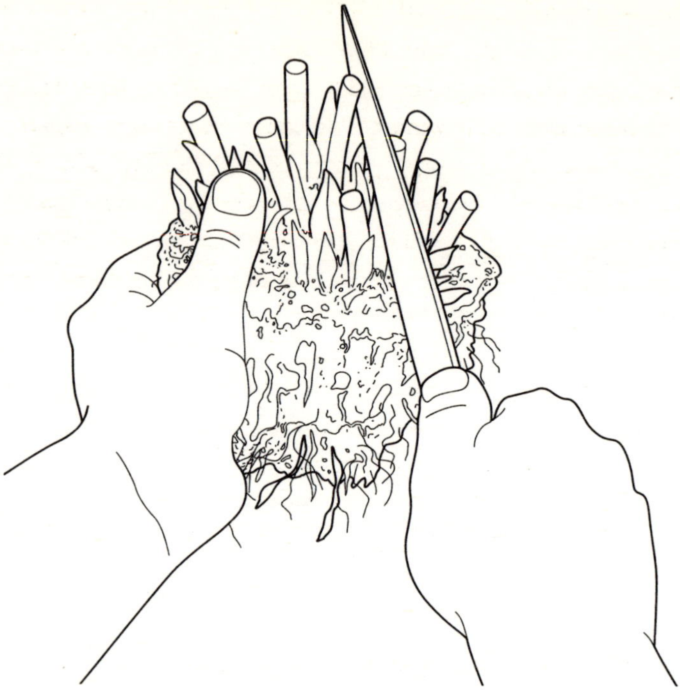

Autumn-flowering perennials (like asters and heleniums) are always divided in spring too, never in autumn. They are likely to die if divided so soon after flowering. Many members of the daisy family (the Asteraceae) form loose clumps. Lift the whole plant, place it on a groundsheet and, using two forks back to back, lever the clump apart. Discard the middle section and use the more vigorous outer pieces. Tighter clump-formers can be chopped into sections with a spade. Aim to get reasonable-sized pieces if replanting back into the ground, and add a slow-release fertilizer (like blood, fish and bone) or bonemeal. The latter is very good for root development. A move to fresh ground also helps vigour. Smaller divisions can be potted up in loam-based compost like John Innes No. 2.

Members of the daisy family can also be raised by cuttings

taken when the fresh growth is 10cm (4in) or so high. Collect them in the cool of the day, trim them under a node, using a one-sided razor blade or clean scalpel, and chop away any large leaves to prevent too much transpiration. Fill clean small pots or seed trays with a free-draining compost with some coarse grit added. Place away from sunlight and keep the cuttings moist – a water-sprayer is useful. Bottom heat also helps speed rooting and a heated propagator is ideal. Once rooted, pinch out the top, and then pot up individually.

Did you know? 'Daisy' is a corruption of 'day's eye' and this indicates that almost all daisies need full sun. Confusingly, the family name comes from '*aster*' which means 'star' in Greek.

SECRETS OF SUCCESS

- Never put up with plants that have a bald patch in the middle – it will show later.
- When dividing, lift plants just as they are surging into growth to lessen the stress.
- If there are long roots (as in sanguisorba), shorten them. This will encourage fine roots to appear.
- Take the outer pieces of large clumps to keep vigour going.
- Replant at the right depth. Look at the soil mark on the stem to gauge this.
- Label carefully.
- Spring is an excellent time to divide most things, but do keep divisions well watered in dry conditions.
- Tap-rooted plants can't be divided: they are propagated by root cuttings taken in late autumn and winter.

Organic Tip ✓

Plant viruses spread through sap. Regular wiping of razor blade, scalpel, secateurs or scissors when propagating, pruning, etc. helps to prevent problems. Flaming the blade with a spirit lamp is the only way to ensure that viruses are killed, but few gardeners go this far.

DIVIDING KNOW-HOW

Hellebores
Divide into large pieces in April, but always make sure you get root with your division. No root means death!

Eryngiums
Some don't and some do. You can divide *Eryngium* x *zabelii* and *E.* x *oliverianum.*

Sanguisorbas
Chop off most of the long roots. Rooting takes place close to the crown of the plant.

Seed-setters
If plants set a lot of seed, they are normally short-lived and difficult to divide. Save the seed instead and sow it when the plant would normally sprinkle its seeds.

4 Cut Back Buddlejas

(mid-April)

KEEPING buddleja plants compact by pruning now helps to maintain vigour because it encourages new growth. Most plants, but not all, respond to hard pruning by reasserting themselves. More modest pruning generally promotes gentler growth. Allowing shrubby plants to get leggier and leggier, or bushier and bushier, usually means fewer flowers and an unattractive plant.

Buddlejas come into the leggy group (mostly) and now is the time to cut back late-summer-flowering buddlejas to strong lower buds. How you prune your buddleja depends on its position. If it's at the back of the border you may want to reduce each stem by half to maintain height. This will give earlier flowers and the plants in front will cover up any unsightly stems. However, if the whole bush is visible, take it back hard so that it stays compact. You may need a pruning saw. Then the new growth will emerge from the base and the main flowering flush will be in late July or August.

Habits vary considerably and colours range from white through to pink, mauve, purple and red-purple. The petals of white-flowered forms tend to brown as they age. Flower spikes vary in size and the fairly diminutive lavender-blue heads of 'Lochinch' fit into a border far better than the whoppers on 'Pink Delight'.

Did you know? The name of the buddleja immortalizes a vicar from Essex, the Rev. Adam Buddle (1662–1715), who collected seaweeds, lichens and wild plants, and died 150 years before the buddleja was actually named by Carl Linnaeus. The species name *davidii* honours the French Jesuit missionary and naturalist Père Armand David, who described it in 1869. It was rediscovered by Dr Augustine Henry (1857–1930) in 1890 in the province of Szechuan and reached Europe in 1893.

Organic Tip ✔

The fragrant buddleja is the best butterfly plant a gardener can grow. In theory it could sustain twenty-two of our native British butterflies because they adore its honey-scented nectar. Flower colour does not seem to matter to butterflies, but buddlejas must be in warm sunshine in order for the nectar to flow.

SECRETS OF SUCCESS

- Hardy buddlejas are trouble-free, adaptable shrubs for sunny, warm positions. They sulk in shade.
- Although they prefer well-drained soil, they do adapt – even performing on acid soil.
- The buddleja has proved an invasive plant. If you take the trouble to dead-head (to prevent unwanted seedlings), you will be rewarded with a far longer flowering season and prevent unwanted seedlings.
- Prune *Buddleja davidii* every year in April.
- Choose a good variety to suit your needs. The new 'Blue Chip' is a patio-sized buddleja suitable for a pot.

VARIETIES

***B.* 'Lochinch' AGM**
A diminutive, compact shrub which keeps lots of silver leaves in winter. Dainty, orange-eyed lavender flowers follow.

***B. davidii* 'Dartmoor' AGM**
Discovered as a seedling, this purple buddleja is unique, having hand-shaped fingers of flowers. You either love it or hate it.

***B. davidii* 'Black Knight' AGM**
Dark purple-black flowers, stunning against the silver foliage.

***B. davidii* 'Royal Red' AGM**
A large plant with very long flowers. Unique red-purple colour.

5 Destroy Slugs and Snails

(late April)

TIME TO hit your slugs and snails, just as they are really beginning to get going. Frisk all hemerocallis, kniphofias and clump-forming iris and destroy any slugs or snails you find before they breed. Lay small plastic flowerpots on their sides in borders to trap more snails, checking them every day or so.

Consider using nematodes (tiny parasitic worms) that attack slugs. Available from garden centres, they come in date-stamped packs that have to be kept in the fridge. Dilute the greyish powdery mix with water, stir well, then apply with a watering can. Target certain areas – where dahlias or hostas will be planted, for instance – because it's too expensive to treat the whole garden, as well as being unnecessary.

The most effective time to water nematodes on is in the late afternoon or early evening when less evaporation takes place. The soil should be damp, so applying them after rainfall is preferable. Afterwards you won't see lots of dead slugs on the surface – all the action takes place underground. One application works for between 4 and 6 weeks and, if the summer is dry, it often clears up the situation. If later problems occur, use the nematodes again in early September.

Did you know? There are slug-eating slugs called shield slugs (*Testacella*), of which there are three species in Britain. Their bodies have small, shell-like plates. Most of us have never seen one, as they live deep in the ground.

Organic Tip ✔

Certain plants are attractive to slugs, while others, particularly aromatic types, aren't. If you use things the slugs really like (such as lettuces and African marigolds), you can lure them away from plants you value highly. Then all you need to do is remove them and destroy them at dusk, when they are at their most active.

SECRETS OF SUCCESS

- Hoe round your garden as much as is possible, as it will disturb the slugs and bring the eggs up to the surface. This makes it easier for birds like robins to eat them.
- Harden off any plants that have been grown in a greenhouse by placing them outdoors on a table for a week, hopefully out of the reach of slugs and snails. This will make them less palatable.
- Don't over-feed plants with nitrogen. It will promote fast, sappy growth that's highly attractive to gastropods.
- Do not use slug bait. One pellet can affect water quality in a small pond. Slugs are an important food in the garden for thrushes, toads and hedgehogs, whose offspring do not do well when fed blue metaldehyde for tea.
- Pick slugs and snails off plants if you need to. Rubber gloves are available to the squeamish.

TYPES OF SLUG

Grey Field Slug (*Derocereas reticulatum*)
The most common and serious slug pest. Usually light grey or fawn, this is the very soft-bodied slug you find in lettuces and cabbages. 3cm (1½in).

Keeled Slug (*Tandonia budapestensis*)
Grey-black with a ridge down the back. These are larger than the Grey Field slug (about 6–7cm/2½in) and they tend to live and feed underground. Potatoes are a delicacy for them.

Black Slug (*Arion ater*)
This is the large slug you are likely to see in the daytime after rain. It can measure up to 20cm (8in) and is black, although some sub-species have a distinctive reddish-brown to yellow colour. This slug cleans up debris, as it feeds on rotting foliage and fungi. Don't kill it.

Garden Slug (*Arion hortensis*)
A slug with tough, leathery skin. Dark in colour (grey–black) with a pale yellowish underside. Destructive at every level, and this one can climb.

6 Divide Erythroniums

(late April)

ERYTHRONIUMS are a delight in April with their Tiffany-lamp flowers, and some have handsome mottled foliage, but the way to get them to spread is to lift them carefully now and replant them in refreshed soil. However, their oval white bulbs are incredibly brittle so this is a 'kid-gloves' task not to be rushed. Lift one clump of bulbs at a time and place it in a bucket. Gently tease the roots apart so that the bulbs can be separated.

Dig over the place where the erythroniums were, then water the patch well. Add blood, fish and bone to replace nutrients, then very carefully dig a hole and replant two or three bulbs straight back into the soil. Move the others to new ground that has already been deeply dug. Water well after planting.

Clumps divided in this way take one year to recover, so do half your clumps one year and the rest the next. Erythroniums, which mainly come from North America, are very hardy and come to life as the snow melts in the same way trilliums do. Some species are very difficult to grow, but named hybrids are often easy. They enjoy friable, fertile soil that retains moisture, but (like many bulbous plants) they resent being waterlogged. Some do set seed, but division is easier.

> **Did you know?** The common name of one non-American species (*Erythronium dens-canis*) is dog's-tooth violet because the bulbs resemble canine teeth. This species is found in an area stretching between Europe, Asia and Japan and it often does well in grassy situations.

Organic Tip ✔

These bulbous plants like friable soil. Adding leaf litter after flowering helps to retain the moisture. Alternatively mulch with bark.

SECRETS OF SUCCESS

- Fertile soil in dappled shade is the ideal for most erythroniums, although some have alpine tendencies.
- They prefer cool, moist springs.
- The hybrids are much easier to grow than trilliums.
- Most species have to be bought in flower because the bulbs tend to be very brittle and easily damaged.
- Leave newly acquired plants undisturbed while flowering, then put them in the ground very gently afterwards.
- Allow them to self-seed.

VARIETIES

***E. californicum* 'White Beauty' AGM**
Creamy flowers blotched in brown at the base, with large, mottled brown-and-green leaves.

***Erythronium* 'Pagoda'**
A starry, yellow-flowered hybrid with slightly mottled leaves. A readily available form, probably the easiest of all and so a good starting point.

***Erythronium* 'Kondo'**
Pallid-yellow flowers with highly reflexed petals that sweep upwards to reveal a red-orange marking.

***E. dens-canis* 'Lilac Wonder'**
Lilac-pink flowers, so swept back that many might think they were cyclamen. They appear in March and their patterned foliage lasts for 5 weeks or so before they retreat underground.

MAY

We should be about to encounter the most perfect gardening moment. Sometime this month you should step outside to a sun-warmed garden burgeoning with life and bathed in early summer light. E. A. Bowles, the distinguished garden writer, put it so much better when he wrote: 'If a fairy godmother or a talking fish offered me three wishes . . . one would have to be to have the clock stopped on a fine morning towards the end of May.' Every committed gardener will applaud his choice. His personal wish was granted: Bowles died on a May day in 1954, one week short of his eighty-ninth birthday.

May is full of foliage, but flowers can be few and far between. It's up to the gardener to fill the May gap with bee-friendly plants, because these essential creatures are in a busy phase and desperately need both nectar and pollen.

1 Take Care of Early-flowering Clematis

(early May)

BY NOW some clematis will have finished or almost finished flowering. These should be left alone, although you can give them a light tidy if needed.

As a general rule, any clematis that flowers before Midsummer's Day will not respond to hard pruning: it may even kill it off. Those that flower after Midsummer's Day should be hard pruned to the lowest buds in spring (see page 40). In between are highly bred, large-flowered clematis: these generally need a sympathetic tidy in spring.

Winter-flowering clematis are mainly evergreens bred from *Clematis cirrhosa*, a species found in warmer parts of Europe. They tend to be leggy and bear pendent white bells with a hint of green. They need warm, south-facing walls and, sometimes in very dry summers, they can drop all their leaves in August; however, they soon revive. Use them to frame windows and doorways.

The elegant C. *armandii*, a Chinese species with large, leathery leaves, bears clusters of fragrant white flowers in spring. It can be rampant and may need restricting, but once established it's a toughie. It often has some brown leaves, but it isn't dying. Just remove them for appearance's sake.

The Atragene Group (containing C. *alpina*, C. *macropetala* and others) flower in April just as the leaves emerge. They need good drainage but make excellent plants for an exposed position. These are slow to establish.

Did you know? Every clematis you buy has instructions on the label according to three pruning groups. Group one is no-prune. Group two is shorten old stems by a quarter and thin shoots in spring. Group three is prune hard in spring. Remove and keep the labels of all clematis so that you can refer to them.

Organic Tip ✔

Clematis are members of the Ranunculaceae, a plant family named after the common frog, Rana temporaria. *Most of the plants in this family (including aconitum, celandine, aquilegia, hellebore and thalictrum) prefer cool roots and moist but well-drained soil. Shield the roots of clematis with a container or a stone slab to create a cool root run. If your garden is dry, avoid growing large-flowered clematis – they will almost certainly suffer from clematis wilt in these conditions. Go for smaller-flowered forms like viticella clematis instead: these are drought-tolerant* *(see page 40)*.

SECRETS OF SUCCESS

- When planting a new clematis, prepare the soil thoroughly and then water well for the first growing season.
- Plant a couple of inches deeper than the level in the pot to protect the crown.
- Support the clematis. Gripple (an easy-to-tension wire system) is excellent.
- If planting an alpina or macropetala, add some grit to the base of the hole to improve drainage.

NO-PRUNE CLEMATIS

C. cirrhosa* var. *balearica
Dark, divided foliage that looks almost black, framing creamy bells lightly spotted in maroon by late January–February.

***C. cirrhosa* var. *purpurascens* 'Freckles' AGM**
Cream flowers, very heavily spotted in berry-red. This clematis can flower before Christmas on a very warm wall.

***C. armandii* 'Apple Blossom' AGM**
A refined form with apple-blossom-pink flowers set against leathery green foliage. All *armandii* types are adored by bees.

C. macropetala
Soft-blue, wispy tutus backed by bright-green foliage.

***C. alpina* AGM**
Single flowers in pink, white or blue made up of four pointed tepals.

***Clematis* 'Brunette'**
Pendent bell-shaped flowers with very thick petals in sombre purple – one of the strongest clematis.

2 Divide Snowdrops and Overcrowded Bulbs

THIS IS an excellent time to divide overcrowded clumps of snowdrops because the bulbs have had a few weeks to replenish their food reserves after flowering. Carefully lift them with a fork, preferably when the soil is damp, and place them on a sheet, then carefully tease the clump apart into ones, twos or threes. Replant again in ones, twos or threes, but try to put some in fresh ground.

If you lift a clump and find that the bulbs are flaccid and limp, it means that they are down on their food reserves. Tell yourself off, then carefully replant the whole clump, mark them with a label or cover them with grit, and water with an organic foliar feed, following packet instructions. Make a note to move them when they are dormant in late August. By then the bulbs should be plumper and firmer and ready to start into growth in early September.

If you remove a clump containing enormous bulbs, each with several flower stems, replant the whole clump. They are in the process of splitting all by themselves; each large bulb is about to subdivide into four or five smaller ones. Make a note to divide them next year instead.

Don't dead-head snowdrops. Many will set seed and sometimes hybrid snowdrops can occur with interesting variations.

Did you know? It is possible to have snowdrops in flower from October until early April. The autumn-flowering snowdrop *Galanthus reginae-olgae* is the earliest. It flowers in October and self-seeds and bulks up well. It was largely distributed by Primrose Warburg, a famous galanthophile who gardened at South Hayes near Oxford. G. 'South Hayes' and G. 'Primrose Warburg', both seedlings from her garden, were named after her death in 1996.

Organic Tip ✔

Regular division and moving snowdrops about encourages them to multiply. Giving them more space allows them to develop bigger bulbs, which leads to more flowers. Regular lifting also helps to prevent fungal diseases like botrytis. As Edward Augustus Bowles (the man credited with inventing the term 'galanthophile') said, 'Stir them up!'

SECRETS OF SUCCESS

- Start with *G. nivalis*, our most common snowdrop. Large colonies occur at religious sites such as Walsingham Abbey in Norfolk and for many years botanists thought it was native. However, it was later found to have been introduced from other parts of Europe, possibly for medicinal reasons.
- Give them dappled shade, close to shrubs and trees, and plant them among non-smothering woodlanders like *Anemone nemorosa*.
- Divide regularly.
- Double forms are petal-packed and always look open, even on the dullest day.
- Feed with blood, fish and bone twice a year, after flowering and in September when they begin to grow again.

EASY AND AVAILABLE SNOWDROPS

***Galanthus* 'Magnet'**
A large, single-flowered hybrid which moves and sways in the garden as if dancing. Strong and vigorous.

***G. nivalis* 'Viridapice'**
A robust snowdrop, larger than *G. nivalis* in every way. The three outer petals are marked in green.

***Galanthus* 'Lady Beatrix Stanley'**
A substantial double, often likened to a large molar tooth. It makes a good garden show.

G. elwesii
A bold snowdrop with grey-green, blunt-tipped leaves and large flowers marked in holly-green. Makes huge bulbs.

3 Sow Half-hardy Seeds under Unheated Glass

(mid-May)

HALF-HARDY annuals need warmth and frost-free conditions, so most gardeners without heated greenhouses are better off sowing them now rather than earlier. They will still have plenty of time to perform and the nighttime temperatures should be ambient. However, daytime temperatures could rise steeply, to over 30°C (90°F) if your greenhouse or cold frame is in an open position. High temperatures prevent germination as effectively as cold nights, so shading is vital. Horticultural fleece (or green netting made for the job) can be used to provide shade; if you have a wooden greenhouse, suspend the fleece from a simple set of cup hooks screwed into the side. Ventilate the greenhouse fully on sunny days, or move the seeds out of full sunlight indoors; if you are using a propagator, always take off the lid.

Seeds have to be able to get moisture, but too much is akin to sitting in a cold bath. Invest in a good watering can with a fine rose and always have the holes pointing upwards so that it delivers a sprinkle rather than a drenching. Fill the watering can from the mains supply and leave it to stand. This brings the water up to room temperature and allows any chlorine to escape. Ideally, watering should be done in the first half of the day.

Tender seeds need extra warmth and germinate much faster if either perlite or vermiculite is added to the compost in a ratio of 50:50. You can also place seed trays inside polystyrene trays to conjure up more warmth.

Did you know? The term 'watering can' first appeared in 1692, in the diary of keen cottage gardener Lord Timothy George of Cornwall. Before then, this French invention was known as a 'watering pot'. In 1886 the Haws watering can was patented by John Haws, who replaced the top-mounted handle with a single round handle at the rear so that it was perfectly balanced. The Haws company still makes the best cans.

SECRETS OF SUCCESS

- Look at the sowing instructions on your seed packet.
- Ventilate your greenhouse to create ambient temperatures. Fitting automatic vents helps.
- Sort out a way of shading your greenhouse.
- Use good loam-based compost because it doesn't dry out like peat-based types. Adding perlite or vermiculite gives extra warmth.
- When pricking out young seedlings, never handle them by the stem. Gently pick them up by one true leaf and lower them into a hole made with a dibber or pencil.
- Pot up seedlings in small round pots, because water congregates in the corners of square pots.
- Pricking out into polystyrene modules makes plants grow faster, so save and wash any that come your way.
- Pricking out seedlings into individual pots (rather than trays) saves disturbing them twice.

Organic Tip ✔

Sow seeds thinly. A mass of seedlings restricts the movement of air, encouraging disease.

HALF-HARDY ANNUALS

***Nicotiana sylvestris* (Tobacco Plant)**
Stately plant that bears a whorl of fragrant, long-trumpeted white flowers. Can reach waist height.

Zinnia
These sun-loving Mexican plants have improved greatly due to better breeding. Varieties vary from the substantial 'Purple Prince' to the smaller 'Aztec Sunshine'. Remove the leading bud for extra flowers.

***Ratibida columnifera* (Mexican Hat Plant)**
The prairie coneflower conjures up summer sun. A sprawling annual with grey foliage and high-coned daisies in yellow and orange.

***Cleome spinosa* (Spider Flower)**
A spiny, rose-pink, purple or white annual that demands hot weather to perform well. Excellent with cosmos and roses.

4 Dead-head Hellebores
(*mid-May*)

CHOICE hybrid hellebores (*Helleborus* × *hybridus*) should be dead-headed now (well before they shed their seed) to prevent unwanted seedlings. Producing seeds takes a lot of energy from a plant and seedlings can swamp choicer plants. In any case, most turn out to be an unattractive muddy colour. Remove the old-flowering stems at the base and tidy up any shabby leaves. Once the plant looks pristine, apply a slow-release fertilizer like blood, fish and bone or powdered chicken manure (sold as 6X). Feed again in early September to keep the plants vigorous.

Keep an eye on hellebore foliage throughout summer because they can suffer from a leaf-spot disease caused by the fungus *Microsphaeropsis hellebori*. Remove any leaves with dark patches as soon as you see them and don't add them to the compost heap. Applying a bark mulch in early autumn helps to prevent spores on the ground from being splashed back up by rain – but don't cover the crown. See also page 171.

Sultry, dark-red astrantias make perfect partners for hellebores. They enjoy the same conditions and they flower as the hellebores fade. However, paler pink astrantias (like 'Buckland') prefer a sunnier position.

Did you know? Double hellebores are a recent innovation, partly prompted by the discovery of two double forms of *H. torquatus* found in Montenegro by Elizabeth Strangman (a famous hellebore breeder) in 1971. The more purple form, which she named 'Dido', was more vigorous than the greener 'Aeneas'. 'Dido' proved a good parent plant and gradually doubles became available.

Organic Tip ✔

If you do find viable hellebore seeds from spent flowers you failed to remove, collect them and sow them immediately. Members of the Ranunculaceae tend to have seeds with a short period of viability. Generally all perennials are best sown when ripe. They usually germinate in the following spring, after a period of cold.

SECRETS OF SUCCESS

- Hellebores enjoy fertile soil with plenty of added organic matter.
- They prefer dappled shade, although they can survive being baked in summer. They don't do well right up against tree trunks – it's too dry and dark.
- These are woodland-edge plants and they need moist but well-drained soil. Mulch with bark or well-rotted organic matter on dry soil, or grow them on mounds if your soil tends to get cold and sticky in winter.
- Try to purchase hellebores that have been grown in an outdoor situation. If you do pick one from a warm greenhouse, keep it somewhere sheltered and plant it out in late spring to lessen the temperature shock.
- Hybrid hellebores come in very deep pots, so you do need to dig deeply when planting.
- Hellebores are often pot-bound when you buy them, with the roots spiralling round. Try to tease the roots out. If this fails, don't be afraid to hack into the roots or to lop off the lower part of the root system, before planting. If you have to take drastic action, water your new plant well for its first growing season.
- Give hellebores plenty of room: they live for decades and make large plants.
- Feed in September; remove all the leaves in December.
- Dead-head after flowering and feed again.

HYBRIDS AND SPECIES

H.* x *hybridus

There are several recognized seed strains, including John Massey's Ashwood Strain and Hugh Nunn's Harvington Strain. White, pale-green and pink show up well in the garden. The slate-blacks can get lost against the bare earth. Wine-red hellebore flowers, though rare, are the most prized. They glow in winter and spring light.

H.* x *ericsmithii

The ordinary Christmas rose is often a miserable plant in the garden. It needs a very well-drained plot to do well and tends to push flowers out at soil level, where they become muddy. However, there are some fine hybrids – although, being hybrids, they do vary in appearance. Typically, *H.* × *ericsmithii* has white flowers tinged with pink set amongst marbled foliage.

H. foetidus

This British native, commonly called the stinking hellebore, combines very dark, divided foliage with small, lime-green bells finely edged in maroon. Best for a wild garden, or in a large woodland garden.

H. argutifolius

The Corsican hellebore needs more space than any other because the stems flop down to the ground like the spokes on a large wagon wheel. The large, apple-green flowers are excellent, but the handsome foliage seems more prone to black spot.

5 The Chelsea Chop and the Effective Thin

(late May)

YOU CAN improve your flower garden later in the year by taking action now. Look at any mature clumps of phlox and thin out the woody stems if they seem too congested. This will give you larger flowers on the remaining stems and it will also allow a better flow of air – hopefully making mildew less likely. Mildew, a water-stress disease, debilitates plants and covers them with white powder. It's unsightly but not life-threatening. Phloxes, monardas and heleniums are prone to it, but they do recover.

Once your phloxes are thinned, wait for a damp, warm day and then mulch them to conserve moisture at the roots. If you are using well-rotted manure or compost, this will add nutrients. However, if you are mulching with partially rotted grass clippings or fine bark, add a slow-release fertilizer (like blood, fish and bone) before mulching because these materials use up nitrogen when decomposing. If you do water phloxes in summer, try to avoid splashing the foliage as this encourages mildew. Carefully tip a can of water on the roots instead.

Plants can also be 'Chelsea chopped' – i.e., cut back by two-thirds – resulting in lusher foliage and later flowers, often on shorter plants. This technique works well with English lavender, campanulas and sedums. Heleniums often suffer from ragged foliage. If they are at the front of the border, reduce the stems at the front by two-thirds, leaving the rest of the stems untouched. The front of the helenium will keep its leaves and flower later, hiding any ragged stems behind it.

Did you know? The Chelsea Flower Show began in 1912 but it's difficult to know when the Chelsea chop began or who started it. If you're brave enough to do it, your garden will shine later in the year. It also works with herbs. The expression probably dates back to the early days of the Chelsea Flower Show, always held in the third week of May. As people were away from their gardens doing the London Season in June and July, and often didn't return home until August, gardeners chopped their plants to delay flowering until their return.

Organic Tip ✔

If your garden is windy, the Chelsea chop will help because shorter plants tend to be sturdier and will need much less staking.

SECRETS OF SUCCESS

- Perform the Chelsea chop only with well-established plants that are looking vigorous, happy and healthy. Choose clump-formers, not spreaders.
- Plants re-shoot from the cut on the stem and this slows them up, so they flower later. Water well in dry conditions to encourage growth.
- English lavender can be cut back in early May to retard the flowers so that they follow on after the first flush of roses – a technique employed at the National Trust's Mottisfont Abbey in Hampshire.
- Varieties of campanula, particularly *C. lactiflora* 'Prichard's Variety' and 'Loddon Anna', can also be treated in this way. Then they will follow the roses rather than coinciding with them.
- Taller sedums can be chopped so that, when the other sedums are in flower, they display fabulous foliage instead.
- Phloxes and delphiniums can also be lopped back by half. Phloxes will flower in early September and blooms will last longer when refreshed by autumn dew. Delphiniums are held back until late summer.

PLANTS SUITABLE FOR CHOPPING

***Helenium* 'Moerheim Beauty' AGM**
A double layer of flouncing petals that form a rust-red–orange skirt with a rich-red petticoat. Rich and sultry. Flowers in late August if chopped. 120cm (4 ft).

***Phlox paniculata* 'Blue Paradise'**
Medium-blue flowers with a dark eye. Stunning in evening light. Up to 60cm (2ft), depending on soil.

***Sedum telephium* (Atropurpureum Group) 'Karfunkelstein' AGM**
Compact variety with smoky-blue, branching foliage. 60cm (2ft) or less.

***Campanula latiloba* 'Highcliffe Variety' AGM**
Not grown as often as it should be, this produces a spire of rich-lavender bells. 120cm (4ft) when chopped.

6 Begin to Put Out Tender Plants

(late May)

THE THIRD week of May is generally considered to be safe enough for tender plants to go outside because the fear of frost has usually passed. However, many professional gardeners wait until mid-June, so if your garden is bleak hold back until then.

If you have a greenhouse and want to plant up a mixed container – making sure it isn't too heavy to move once planted – arrange and pot up frost-tender plants. They will have 3 weeks to mingle together before going outside and they will look much better for it. The added warmth under glass will allow them to grow quickly and by mid-June there should be less of a gap between nighttime and daytime temperatures.

When potting up, use a loam-based compost such as John Innes No. 3, which retains moisture and contains lots of nutrients. Water all the plants well before planting and, once planted, keep the compost damp but not wet. This will encourage root development. Feed regularly with a potash-rich plant food to encourage flowering – tomato feed is ideal. Never use a nitrogen-rich feed: it produces soft, leafy growth that is highly attractive to molluscs. Dead-head regularly.

Impatiens, fuchsias and solenostenum (previously coleus) do best in shade. However, most tender plants love sunshine and warmth. If watering is a problem, opt for drought-tolerant pelargoniums, petunias or succulents.

Did you know? Hardiness is a very difficult thing to assess. By the late eighteenth century, camellias, which were introduced from Japan and China, were being grown in opulent orangeries in the belief that they were considered tender. They were seen as a status symbol, but they were considered difficult to keep alive. In 1814 some were left outside by mistake and were found to be completely hardy. This was recorded by Samuel Curtis in his *Botanical Magazine*. As a result, English nurserymen began to breed them and soon the camellia was popular in Victorian gardens.

Organic Tip ✔

Soft-stemmed plants like dahlias, nasturtiums, begonias and solenostemon are first to succumb to frost because it is able to penetrate them easily. The freezing and thawing of the sap ruptures the plant's cells. Woodier-stemmed plants like pelargoniums are much tougher: they suffer cold conditions in the rugged terrain of their native South Africa.

SECRETS OF SUCCESS

- Harden off all plants that come from the protection of the greenhouse or the garden centre by placing them outside for a week. This allows them to acclimatize and hardens up the foliage, making it less attractive to slugs and snails.
- Position plants carefully. Aromatic plants have an oily covering that allows them to avoid heatstroke. Succulents carry water. Both are happy in a south-facing hotspot. Even so, they will still need water and food. Silver-leaved plants are also sun-lovers.
- Impatiens and small-flowered begonias prefer shade. Solenostemon, and most golden-leaved plants, also prefer shade.
- Try to keep plants away from the wind: it distresses most soft-leaved plants greatly. Find sheltered niches.
- If using containers, remember to water even on wet days.
- Feed regularly, using home-made comfrey tea (see page 103) or liquid tomato feed.
- Terracotta gets very warm at the root, but the effects can be lessened by dropping a slightly smaller plastic pot inside the terracotta one. However, the gap may become a home for slugs – so be vigilant.
- When choosing containers, avoid those with over-hanging lips – they shelter slugs and snails.

JUNE

June satisfies the hedonist in us all. It's the month when once-and-only flowering roses drip with bloom and, when they provide such glory, it's not surpising that they don't perform again. The repeat-flowerers are a little later and they ration their flowers out over 4 months. But it's those exuberant once-and-onlies that capture the abundance of June and make it such a special time.

Blowsy peonies with evocative French names open fully, while philadelphus and honeysuckle scent the evening air. Most gardens look their best in June: the challenge is to extend them into autumn with a whole range of frost-tender plants and hardy prairie plants and grasses.

1 Make a Sand Tray

(early June)

THE GARDEN is now full of verdant new growth and inevitably there will be moments when you hear the heart-rending snap of stem or flower. Don't think of it as a tragedy. If it's a flower, relegate it to a small posy vase placed somewhere shady. If it's a stem, it may well make a new plant.

The easiest propagation method is to have ready-filled seed trays of damp horticultural sand waiting to plunge any casualties into. Small seed trays are ideal and can accommodate forty small snippets. Alternatively, you can make a dedicated wooden frame, either on the greenhouse floor or somewhere shady outdoors away from cats. A bucket also works. Keep the sand damp throughout the year. In cool conditions cuttings take months to root, but in warm weather it's a matter of weeks.

You can use your sand trays for deliberate cuttings of short-lived perennials and silver-leaved plants like lavenders, artemisias, salvias, anthemis, achilleas, penstemons, pelargoniums, thymes, dianthus, rock roses and euphorbias. The technique is to find new growth that has just started to harden but is still pliable. Remove the lower leaves and any flowers or buds, trim beneath the bumpy node and plunge the bottom two-thirds of the cutting into the sand. Remember to label.

Did you know? Most cuttings root easily if trimmed below the leaf joint, but moist conditions and warmth speed up the process. As the year wears on, cuttings take a lot longer to root and early September is a good cut-off point. Any cuttings taken in September should be left alone until late spring, unless put into a heated propagator.

Organic Tip ✔

Take cuttings in the cool of the day and place them in polythene bags with dampened kitchen paper. Label as you go. If you have very tender plant cuttings, surround them with hardier plants as protection. If you are trying to root more challenging plants (like daphnes), add a couple of easier plants (such as sages) because the developing roots of the sage will keep the sand warm and well drained – encouraging difficult cuttings to root.

PLANTS EASILY RAISED FROM CUTTINGS

All silver-leaved plants can be raised easily from cuttings

Dianthus (Pinks)
Non-flowering shoots taken in summer root very easily.

Salvias
Most (hardy and tender) can be raised easily from cuttings.

Penstemons
These are incredibly easy.

Pelargoniums
Take cuttings in August and throw away old leggy plants so that you can start again in spring. Some gardeners leave the cuttings on their workbench for a day so that the cut ends callous over before plunging them into sand.

Succulents
These are mainly easy to take, but again some gardeners allow the cuttings a day to callous over. Succulent cuttings can be left on a bench for weeks.

SECRETS OF SUCCESS

- Find new growth that has begun to harden up – known as semi-ripe.
- Keep cuttings in warm positions, but out of direct sunlight.
- Always trim any very large leaves to prevent excessive transpiration.
- Use a large nail or pencil to make a hole in the sand for your cuttings.
- Plunge the cuttings in deeply so that two-thirds are submerged.
- Many plants do not need hormone rooting powder.
- Cover cuttings with a polythene bag for the first 10 days to prevent moisture loss through the leaves.
- Once your cuttings have rooted, pot them up into gritty compost. A gentle tug usually tells you if roots are present.
- Keep cuttings on the dry side over winter and fleece them in cold weather.

2 Clip Box
(early June)

BOX IS A slow-growing British native tree that thrives on well-drained hills. However, few mature trees survive owing to the past popularity of this hard wood for box-making. The best specimens are found at Chequers, the Prime Minister's country home in the Chilterns. Most box grown in gardens is clipped into tight shapes. Because they are so slow-growing, a once-a-year cut is enough to keep them looking neat.

In grand country-house gardens the traditional time to clip the box parterre and topiary was always Derby Day (in early June) when the entire family was away at the races. It's good timing. The fear of frost has passed and, once clipped, the box will respond with a flush of new growth, so will look green and lively during the summer.

You may not aspire to a full parterre or knot garden, but many gardeners have some clipped box shapes. These should be snipped and clipped now. A pair of one-handed shears (loosely based on old-fashioned sheep shears) is the ideal tool. Use a groundsheet to catch all the debris.

Clipping probably takes a few minutes per box bush, but the real work starts once you've finished, because every tiny snippet of cut leaf needs to be teased away from the plant. Decomposing foliage could rot down in the heart of the bush and set off fungal disease. This preening takes longer than the clipping itself, but good husbandry will help to prevent box blight (*Cylindrocladium buxicola*), a lethal fungal disease.

Did you know? Topiary is an ancient skill practised since Roman times. Pliny the Younger (*c*.AD 61–112) describes the elaborate figures of animals and obelisks found in a Tuscan villa owned by Cneius Matius Calvena, a friend of Julius Caesar. Calvena is credited with inventing topiary and the Latin word for an ornamental gardener was *topiarius*.

Organic Tip ✔

Damp, overcast days are ideal for trimming box and yew because the exposed new growth can scorch in hot sun. The wood is also less resinous on damp days, but when clipping wipe the blades of your shears with a damp cloth to keep them sharp and clean.

SECRETS OF SUCCESS

- Clipping box continually exhausts the plants, so all box bushes grown in the ground should be fed in spring and autumn to keep the foliage a rich green.
- Potted box needs a fortnightly nitrogen-rich foliar feed, or the foliage will turn yellow and look more like an olive tree.
- Ready-made topiary is expensive, but the process takes years. Many topiarized shapes are wired with metal stakes and, as the bush grows, sometimes this wire cuts in and strangles part of the plant. If this happens, snip away the dead area and loosen the wire.
- Box blight can be more prevalent on tunnel-grown plants produced in warm, muggy conditions. Either raise your own cuttings or buy from a specialist British nursery that produces box trees in the open air.
- A further trim can be given to box topiary in August to smarten it up ready for winter.

VARIETIES FOR TOPIARY

Buxus sempervirens **'Suffruticosa'**
This rich-green, small-leaved box is the most common variety used in topiary.

B. sempervirens **'Elegantissima'**
A variegated box with ivory-white and green leaves. Good in bright sunlight.

B. sempervirens **'Faulkner'**
Larger-leaved, bright-green box that is still suitable for clipping.

B. sempervirens **'Latifolia Maculata'**
Bright-yellow young leaves. Brightens up a shady area.

B. sempervirens **'Rotundifolia'**
Larger, oval green leaves.

3 Plant Agapanthus and Other Borderline-hardy Ornamentals

(mid-June)

ALL TOO often gardeners are tempted into planting frost-tender or borderline-hardy perennials (including salvias, fuchsias, agapanthus and penstemons) in late summer or early autumn when they look at their most magnificent in garden centres. This often leads to failure because the plant never has enough time to establish a good root system before winter sets in. However, if planted now they stand a much better chance of shrugging off bad weather – although sometimes they will not reappear until the following June.

Agapanthus provide a vibrant blast of blue when much of the garden is full of golden yellows. The plant is native to South Africa, where it grows throughout the Cape. About twenty forms grow in the wild, including subspecies, but plant breeders have selected and bred many types to create hundreds of named varieties. Deciduous forms come from areas of the eastern Cape that have rain in summer and dry winters, often with frost. They are hardy. Evergreen forms hail from the western Cape, where it rains either in winter or all year round. They are less hardy. Named forms usually have a deciduous or evergreen tendency, but not always.

The best for outdoor planting are deciduous varieties. They are hardier than you think and if planted in well-drained ground can survive very hard winters. All agapanthus prefer full sun. It is a myth that agapanthus grown in pots perform better if starved of food and water. They like rich, moist soil, so water regularly and feed fortnightly with a potash-rich liquid (like tomato feed) or comfrey tea (see page 103) from May until September. They don't mind crowding – re-pot them every 4–6 years in April and divide them then too.

Did you know? The long, unpleasant winter of 1963 was an eye-opener for nurserymen. Many plants previously thought to be very tender survived, causing opinions about them to be revised.

SECRETS OF SUCCESS WITH BORDERLINE-HARDY PLANTS

- Many people imagine plants to be better protected if grown in a pot. In reality, potted plants are more vulnerable in winter weather than those in the ground. For the greatest chance of success, begin to dry the pot off in late September by reducing watering. Lay the pot on its side or stand it on pot feet.
- Make use of your microclimates. South-facing walls can support tender plants that could be difficult elsewhere.
- A potash-rich feed throughout summer also hardens and toughens the foliage.
- Gravel gardens help plants to survive. The gravel filters the water in winter and acts as a mulch. In summer, heat rises off the gravel or small pebbles and is thrown back up on the plant, ripening the wood. It also conserves moisture and many plants from warm places enjoy heavy summer rainfall.
- Mulch tender plants in the garden with a thick layer of bark or bracken.
- If a plant disappears, give it 6 months to reappear from the base before you dig it up.

Organic Tip ✔

Potted agapanthus can be overwintered outside as long as they are kept dry. Place the pots in the lee of a wall and store them on their sides so that water cannot penetrate. Lay an old blanket (or horticultural fleece or bubble wrap) over them in very cold weather.

VARIETIES OF BORDERLINE-HARDY PLANTS TO TRY IN SHELTERED PLACES

***Melianthus major* AGM (Honey Bush)**
The ultimate foliage plant, with huge jagged leaves in grey-green. Find a hotspot against a south-facing wall and this substantial South African plant will amaze you by reappearing every year. It may even flower, producing a blood-red spike, if happy.

***Euphorbia mellifera* AGM**
An exotic, ebullient spurge from the Azores. A waist-high herbaceous plant with emerald-green foliage and rust-brown, honey-scented flowers that can fragrance the February air. The sap is an irritant.

***Trachelospermum jasminiodes* AGM (Star Jasmine)**
An evergreen fragrant climber bearing clusters of white flowers. A large shrub for a sheltered position against a warm wall.

Buddleja agathosma
Large, silver, serrated leaves and fragrant violet flowers that appear just before the leaves. Another large shrub for a warm wall.

4 Prune Early-summer Shrubs

(mid-June)

PRUNE all early-summer flowering shrubs like philadelphus, deutzia and kolkwitzia now. They flower on the previous year's wood, so you need to preserve most of the older wood whilst also encouraging some new growth for next year's flowers. Generally, the technique is to remove one-third of the old wood straight after flowering. Shape the bush as well, if needed.

Philadelphus varieties vary greatly in habit from the lanky and tall to the twiggy and compact. If you are pruning a vigorous grower, it is often best to remove one in four branches from the base using a Felco pruning saw. If it's a compact variety, like *Philadelphus* × *lemoinei* 'Manteau d'Hermine' AGM, prune very lightly. One of the most accommodating medium-sized summer-flowering shrubs is *P.* × *lemoinei* 'Belle Etoile' AGM. Each citrus-scented white flower is blotched in the centre with a touch of maroon, a colour that flatters dark roses and peonies.

Pruning also depends on the maturity and size of the shrub. Newly planted specimens are best left alone. It's also best to be gentle on youngsters that are at the start of their lives. Just remove any straggling or weak stems at this stage, if needed.

Old, overgrown lilacs and other shrubs need a 3-year strategy to rejuvenate them. Cut away one complete third by pruning back the stems at the base now. Take another third next June and tackle the remaining piece in the third year.

Did you know? Although syringa is, correctly, the name for lilac, it is also often applied to philadelphus. It derives from the Greek *syrinx*, meaning pipe, and, as the stems of both these shrubs are hollow and could be used in pipe-making, the name was used for both. Gardeners constantly get confused by having two very different groups of plants known by the same name.

SECRETS OF SUCCESS

- Most early-summer flowering shrubs need a warm position and good drainage.
- Invest in a good pair of secateurs, loppers and a pruning saw. Keep them sharp and don't leave them outside.
- Don't be secateur-happy. Stand back and look at the whole plant from a distance before starting to prune. When you know what you are going to do, take it slowly. The ideal is to create an open framework.
- Feed and mulch after pruning all shrubs. Sprinkle blood, fish and bone or a chicken-manure product (as instructed by the manufacturer), then mulch with bark or well-rotted grass clippings to keep the moisture in the ground.

EARLY-SUMMER SHRUBS

***Deutzia* x *hybrida* 'Strawberry Fields' AGM**

This close relative of philadelphus has clusters of starry flowers and this pink-and-white flowered form is very pretty in June. Can survive in some shade.

***Kolkwitzia amabilis* 'Pink Cloud' AGM (Beauty Bush)**

Prefers full sun and lives up to its common name of Beauty Bush. Clear-pink, bell-shaped flowers.

***Philadelphus* 'Beauclerk' AGM (Mock Orange)**

White flowers with the merest hint of crimson-pink at the centre of each.

***Weigela florida* 'Foliis Purpureis' AGM**

Dark, smoky foliage and dark-pink, trumpet-shaped flowers.

Organic Tip ✔

Pruning is rather like kicking someone: it promotes a reaction. The harder you kick, the more reaction you get. Hard pruning promotes vigorous vegetative growth. Light pruning, back to the leading branches, promotes gentle growth and flower.

5 Divide Bearded Irises

(late June)

EVERY GARDEN should contain some bearded irises – the ones with grey-green leaves, strong stems and fragrant frilly flowers. They are divided into six categories according to height, which varies greatly. The shortest bearded irises of all, miniature dwarf, generally reach 20cm (8in) and flower in April. The tall bearded irises, which reach 1 metre (39in), are the last group to flower. They peak between mid-May and mid-June, depending on variety. Gardeners should exploit this breadth, as it's possible to have iris flowers for 10 weeks of the year.

Bearded irises need a sunny situation and well-drained soil to do well. The shortest kinds can be left undivided for several years and still perform. However, tall bearded irises should be divided every third year, 2 weeks after flowering.

The technique is the same for all. Lift the rhizomes, discarding the older pieces and keeping the firm, plumped-up, paler pieces. Then trim the leaves back to just above the point where they begin to fan out; this should reduce transpiration and prevent wind rock. Replant the pieces in soil which has had some organic matter added, but don't overdo the feeding. Leave the top of the rhizome visible – rather like a crocodile in a lake. The rhizome needs baking, so it should face the sun.

Did you know? Iris was the Greek goddess of the rainbow, able to travel between heaven and earth, and irises are still planted on Greek graves. The iris also symbolized eloquence; the flower adorning the Sphinx's head is believed to be an iris.

Organic Tip ✔

Bearded irises produce large, long rhizomes that need to be exposed to sunlight. Never hem them in with other plants: they need space to shine. Some remontant varieties re-flower in September.

VARIETIES OF TALL BEARDED IRIS

'Braithwaite'
A two-tone blue iris with velvety navy-blue falls and pale-blue standards.

'Jane Phillips'
A pale-blue self (all one colour).

'Edith Wolford'
A softly ruffled pale yellow and pastel violet-blue.

'Dusky Challenger'
A ruffled dark iris – one of the best.

'Jesse's Song'
An informal white-and-violet ruffled iris.

'Rajah'
Bright-yellow standards supported by maroon-brown falls marbled in white veins close to the beard. Sophisticated.

SECRETS OF SUCCESS

- Full sun and good drainage are essential.
- When planting a new iris, soak the rhizomes in water for an hour, then place them in a position where they will get as much sun as possible.
- Space each rhizome 22–30cm (9–12in) apart and almost cover it with soil, leaving the upper part exposed. Firm in and water well.
- Feed in the spring with a top-dressing of a general fertilizer. A second top-dressing of bonemeal can be applied after flowering if you wish.
- Once established, irises should not be watered or over-fed. Over-feeding encourages rotting.
- Remove any browned leaves during the growing season to discourage leaf spot.
- Cut off the flowering stems at the base once the flowers have faded.

6 Get the Scissors Busy

(late June)

TEN MINUTES spent with a small pair of scissors, preferably ones with easy-to-locate brightly coloured handles, will reap great rewards. First snip off any unwanted seed heads from spring performers like aquilegia, Welsh poppy, the dark cow parsley (*Anthriscus sylvestris* 'Ravenswing'), hellebores and the white stock (*Matthiola incana alba*). This will prevent unwanted seeding, saving much work next year. It will also reinvigorate your plant and make it live longer. Some plants – like white stock – die if they are allowed to set seed.

Give a short back and sides to spent violas, pulmonarias and perennial wallflowers as they finish flowering. Many violas will perform again in early autumn. Stocks and wallflowers will remain vigorous and compact for next year. Use cut material for cuttings, if needed. Shear off early hardy geraniums and campanulas too. Then remove all faded flowers to improve the look of the border. This will promote a longer flowering season and some plants (like heleniums and valerian) will produce months of value.

Annuals will also carry on until autumn if meticulously dead-headed, although after August it's worth letting some early-flowering annuals set seed. Once ripe, collect the seeds at noon on dry, sunny days. Place the heads in paper bags (or large envelopes) and add a plant label straight away. Clean and store away from mice – a tin in the shed is ideal. Don't dismiss annuals as a waste of time. They are easy and they satisfy insects and bees more than most other plants.

Dead-head weigela and buddleja flowers as soon as they fade as this will encourage later flowers. Also dead-head perpetually flowering perennials (anthemis, knautia, helenium, phlox and valerian, for instance) to keep them in flower for months.

CUT-AND-COME-AGAIN FLOWERS

Dahlias
Pick newly opened flowers and they will last for a week in a cool position.

Roses
Cut in the early morning, choosing buds that are about half open. Strip the stems of the lower leaves and snip the bottom. Plunge them up to their necks in cold water and add a commercial flower food. Keep them in a cool place away from direct sunlight.

Scabious
Any scabious makes an excellent cut flower.

Sweet Peas
Summery and scented. Picked every other day, they will carry on for weeks. Stand for 2–3 hours in a bucket of water in a cool place outdoors so that the pollen beetles fly away.

Did you know? Seeds found on archaeological digs are often carbon-dated. Two of these ancient seeds have subsequently germinated. The oldest is a 2,000-year-old date palm seed recovered from excavations at Herod the Great's palace at Masada in Israel. The next oldest is a 1,300-year-old seed from the sacred lotus (*Nelumbo nucifera*) that was recovered from a dry lake bed in north-eastern China.

Organic Tip ✔

Saving your own seeds is a carbon-friendly process and organizations like the Hardy Plant Society and the Cottage Garden Society have free seed-exchange schemes that heavily reward donors.

SECRETS OF SUCCESS

- Use a pair of kitchen scissors and snip into the stems as low as possible, angling the cut sharply downwards so that the stem is much less visible in the border.
- Annual seeds need storing until they are sown next spring. The secret of storing them well is to make sure that the seeds are really ripe and dry.
- Perennial plant seed is best sown straight away because most perennial seeds need a period of cold (or vernalization) before germinating. A simple cold frame is the best position once sown. Some seeds take more than one year to germinate.
- A covering of grit (on seeds that are likely to take their time) helps to keep the moisture in.
- Pick cut-and-come-again flowers regularly.

JULY

Although the main growth spurt is over for the year, the balmy nights of high summer make perfect growing conditions for tender plants like dahlias, salvias and exotic cannas. These are the plants that are going to carry the garden on towards a glorious finale, so watering, feeding and dead-heading them now will pay great dividends later.

The earlier-flowering perennials are well and truly over, so they will be looking shabby and their seed heads may be browning. July is the month to remove any signs of brown, be they seeding plants, shabby leaves or wind-damaged foliage. Brown is an autumn colour: it can look glorious in September when the garden wears a decadent air and resembles an old lady in bling, but summer should be fresh, full of sun-washed colour. It's a soft, watercolour season.

1 Rose Care

(early July)

THE FIRST flush of roses is over and it's time to reward your hungry plants with a rose food that contains nitrogen for leaf, phosphorous for root and potash for flower. Rose feeds are generally rich in potash (as you would expect) to encourage flower rather than foliage, and this is one plant food you should invest in. A general-purpose fertilizer has evenly balanced helpings of all three which will promote too much soft leaf.

Feeding roses should be a regular affair. Potash given in February hardens the wood. Feed them with general rose fertilizer in April and then again in July. Then stop and allow the rose to slow down naturally. Always follow the instructions on the box to the letter and weigh if necessary. Usually it's about 60g per square metre (2½oz per square yard).

Repeat-flowering roses will need dead-heading. This is one of the most soothing pastimes, the sort of thing you nip out and do every couple of days. It pays dividends. However, remember that the lower you take the cut, the more time the plant will take to produce another flush. There is no earthly point in dead-heading once-and-only flowering roses. Leave these well alone and some will form hips.

Once-and-only roses should not be shunned by the gardener: they flower gloriously in June, bearing lots of blooms. Repeat-flowering roses come in flushes, with quite a long gap between. Perpetual-flowering roses ration their flowers quite meanly. Call me a hedonist, but I love once-and-onlies.

Did you know? The earliest roses grown in Europe flowered just once, in June. However, some Chinese species are repeat-flowering and one, 'Old Blush', introduced into Europe in the late eighteenth century, has the common name of the Monthly Rose. It bears semi-double, silver-pink flowers with a sweet-pea fragrance and its upright branches are almost thorn-free. It was probably cultivated in China before the tenth century. Its arrival in the West signalled a new quest for repeat-flowering varieties.

Organic Tip ✔

Simply bred roses are disease-free, and gallicas, rugosas and ramblers are bomb-proof and ideal for the organic gardener. If a rose flowers only once, plant a viticella clematis nearby to extend the flowering season (see page 40).

SECRETS OF SUCCESS

- Feed roses well: this allows them a much greater chance of fending off disease.
- Opt for healthy varieties and buy them from rose specialists who can advise you about which to plant.
- Plant your roses carefully. The best method is to plant bare-root varieties during their dormant spell. These are dispatched between October and late February. Make sure the soil is frost-free when planting.
- Container-grown roses in flower need carefully nurturing during their first growing season. Plant them well, then water and feed them to avoid plant stress.
- Correct pruning is essential (see page 21).

TOP VARIETIES OF ONCE-AND-ONLY ROSES

Gallica Rose 'Surpasse Tout'
Fragrant, rich-carmine, semi-double flowers on a compact, upright bush.

Rambling Rose 'Goldfinch'
Clusters of small apricot flowers that fade to cream. A moderately vigorous rambler with small, light-green foliage. Captures early summer.

Rambling Rose 'Paul's Himalayan Musk'
A rose that's best climbing through a tree. Smothered with clusters of pale-pink pompom flowers.

Climbing Rose 'Mme Grégoire Staechelin'
An exceptionally vigorous rose with large pink flowers. Each petal has a darker reverse, and pear-shaped hips follow. Also has wonderful foliage.

2 Summer-prune Wisteria

(early July)

ESTABLISHED wisterias need summer-pruning once the long, whippy shoots reach about 60cm (2ft) in length. Cut this season's side growths back to four or six leaves towards the ripened wood. Keep the shoots this length until autumn, if possible. Once the plant is dormant you will need to prune again in February or early March (leaving just two buds) so that you create a skeletal framework. This twice-yearly pruning regime lets in more light to ripen the wood and encourages more flowering spurs and fat flower buds. After a good summer your wisteria should drip with bloom every spring. A twice-yearly prune will also keep the plant compact, making it less prone to wind damage should gales occur.

If you are still training a young wisteria to its full height or breadth, leave the leading shoots alone but tie them in now. Once the desired height or breadth is reached, you can begin pruning in the established way. Watch the sap, though: it stains clothing a rusty brown. If you are restoring an overgrown wisteria and have to remove whole parts of the plant, February is the best time.

Did you know? Chinese wisterias (*Wisteria sinensis*) and Japanese (*W. floribunda*) twine in different directions. Japanese wisteria twines clockwise and Chinese wisteria twines anticlockwise. A good way to remember is to form the letters from the top and then follow them round: the letter J turns clockwise, whilst C goes anticlockwise. *W. sinensis* produces its flowers on bare wood. *W. floribunda*, however, has leaves and flowers at the same time.

Organic Tip ✔

Wisterias have pea flowers (as do laburnums) because they belong to the legume family. They should not be given extra nitrogen. They fix their own at the root. It will make them too leafy, at the expense of flower, and it could scorch the roots.

SECRETS OF SUCCESS

- Buy your wisteria in flower from a good nursery, making sure that the flowers are a good colour and of good size.
- Choose a named and grafted plant. Look for the visible bulge of the graft union near the base of the stem and keep this above the ground. Seed-raised wisterias are variable and unreliable flowerers.
- Choose a plant that is 120cm (4ft) tall, as these are cheaper and easier to establish.
- Find a sunny position and plant in well-drained, fertile soil. Keep your new plant watered for the first 2 years during dry periods.
- If you are planting it close to a wall, make sure that it is 60cm (2ft) away.
- Do not fertilize young wisterias.
- Late frosts can harm the newly emerging shoots at a vulnerable stage. For this reason, it's always advisable to avoid east-facing walls where harsh morning sun causes a damaging quick thaw.

VARIETIES

***Wisteria* 'Caroline'**
Grey-blue, scented flowers even on young plants. A popular wisteria for training along wires or up a trellis against a sunny house wall or fence.

***W. floribunda* 'Alba' AGM**
A white form with pointed racemes of flower.

***W. floribunda* 'Multijuga' AGM (syn. 'Macrobotrys')**
Attractive green foliage and long, mauve-lilac, fragrant racemes over 60cm (2ft) in length.

***W. sinensis* 'Amethyst'**
Deep violet-purple, scented flowers. Compact in shape.

3 Mulch and Water

(mid-July)

YOUR LAWN may well be looking bare and brown. However, when rain does fall lawns recover within a week and soon green up, so don't waste mains water irrigating the grass – enjoy the weather instead. Concentrate on containers: they need watering every day because rain fails to penetrate the leafy canopy – even on wet days. Also water newly planted trees, roses, clematis, shrubs and perennials – even those that have been in the ground for 3–4 months. Don't dribble the hose on them. Fill up buckets of water and gently tip them on without disturbing the roots. Two buckets a week per plant is usually enough.

Often plants in trouble angle their leaves almost vertically downwards to avoid transpiration. Witch hazels (hamamelis) always do this. Water copiously, because like many Asian plants witch hazels are used to a rainy season in summer; this will make a lot of difference to next year's flowers.

If the ground gets damp after a night's rain, mulch any plants that enjoy moisture. Partially rotted grass clippings are ideal. Put the clippings on a sheet and leave them to brown for a day or two. Turn the heap and leave again, then layer the brown clippings on to damp soil. They will keep in moisture but soon rot down. If you're using bark (which rots down slowly, using up nitrogen as it does so), add a balanced sprinkle of slow-release fertilizer first – blood, fish and bone is ideal. Finally, order some water butts. Get these bulky items delivered – they are not at all car-friendly.

Did you know? Comfrey 'Bocking 14' has unusually high levels of plant nutrients in its leaves. What is more, the proportions of nutrients are almost identical to those in commercial tomato foods. A patch of 'Bocking 14' planted around your compost heap can be made into comfrey tea. Chop a few handfuls of leaves and put them in a container with a weight on top. After a few days a brown liquid will emerge. Dilute this, 1 part tea to 20 parts water, and use.

VARIETIES OF MULCH

Bark

This material looks wonderful in woodland borders. It rots down slowly, so you always need to apply a nitrogen-based fertilizer to compensate for the nitrogen lost from the soil during the decomposition process. Buy a good-quality bark. If in doubt, buy and examine one bag. Take it back and complain if you discover that it is made from wood offcuts.

Garden Compost

Good round shrubs and trees where you can hoe, because seedlings will appear. If you want to use your own compost, avoid putting any seeding weeds on to your heap. Also avoid copious seeders like foxgloves and aquilegias.

Gravel and Pebbles

The best material for hot areas of the garden. Buy it locally so that it matches your soil; if you need a lot, get it from a building supplier. Sizes vary. Pea gravel is so fine it can tread into the house on animal paws. Gravel or pebbles will need replacing every third or fourth year.

Well-rotted Animal Manure

A very hard commodity to get hold of and recently discredited due to residues of aminopyralid, a hormone-type weedkiller. Get it only from someone who feeds their animals on home-grown silage and hay. Only then can they verify its safety.

Organic Tip ✔

If your compost turns sticky due to too many grass clippings, partially decomposing them for a day or two before adding them helps enormously. Otherwise, incorporate 'browns' such as stems, dead flower heads or even scrunched-up cardboard.

SECRETS OF SUCCESS WITH WATERING

- If you have well-drained soil, set up an irrigation system in early spring. Use a timer if necessary. Remove it in autumn.
- Seep hoses deliver a fine spray from their sides. They work well as long as there are no kinks or sharp bends.
- Porous hoses can be snaked round the garden, as they exude water from all the way round their circumference. They can also be buried to a depth of 10cm (4in).
- Sprinklers are adaptable because you can move them, but avoid using them for certain crops. Some (such as potatoes) are prone to disease if their foliage gets wet.
- Keep water butts, as many as you can place, but use this water on larger plants. It can encourage damping off (a fungal disease) if watered on to seedlings.
- Seedlings need tapwater. This should stand in a watering can for several hours to reach air temperature and to allow the chlorine from mains water to escape. Every time you empty a can, fill it up again.
- Watering near dusk encourages slugs, so try to avoid this.

4 Save Seeds

(mid-July)

ALTHOUGH it's best to dead-head annuals, dahlias and any other perpetually flowering plants in order to encourage more flowers, this means that you won't get seeds. Now is the time to consider allowing some plants to set seed. Many choice garden plants produce seeds readily and it's possible to collect them.

Gather together old paper bags and envelopes, a pencil, scissors and plastic labels. Collect ripe seed heads in the middle of the day, if possible, as they are likely to be much drier then. Write the label, pop them in a bag and store; the seed heads will gradually shrivel and crack to release their seeds. Then clean the debris off the seeds and put them in a sealed envelope with the label. Store them in a tin in a cool shed with some silica sachets – the type found in the packaging when you buy a handbag or electrical gadgets.

This is a cost-effective way of gardening, especially now that commercial packets are expensive and often contain few seeds. Later in the year, let some of your late-season annuals produce seeds too – including nicotiana and cosmos. Annual seeds happily germinate after storage. Hardy annual seeds (like cornflower, ammi and calendula) can be sown in autumn and overwintered in a frame for earlier flowering. More often the seeds of annuals are stored and sown in March or April. Perennial seeds, however, are best sown immediately and placed somewhere cool, although they may not germinate until they have had a period of stratification – a wintry cold snap. Aquilegia and smyrnium are best scattered directly on the ground if you need more: they're difficult to grow in pots.

Did you know? A single field poppy can produce up to 60,000 seeds (according to the Royal Botanic Gardens at Kew), so there could be millions of seeds in a field. The seeds can remain viable for at least 40 years and they germinate when exposed to light. So if you've sprinkled seeds that have failed to germinate, stir up the soil and see if it helps.

Organic Tip ✔

If you've got dry shade where little else seems to grow, try tipping on spare seeds. You might include honesty and aquilegia – these tap-rooted plants often succeed if allowed to develop slowly over winter. Cyclamen seeds can also get a grip. As the seedlings develop, they improve the soil structure and allow you to plant other things in this difficult spot.

SECRETS OF SUCCESS

- The key to saving seeds is to make sure that they are fully ripe. At this stage the seed pods will look dry and show signs that they are about to crack open. Do not delay: seeds are dispersed rapidly when they are fully ripe and you may miss your chance. Ripe seeds are viable seeds.
- Save only the seeds you need. A carrier bag full of foxglove seeds is a waste of time unless you have a million friends to give them to.
- Harvest when the seeds are dry and always label as you snip.
- Clean the seeds on a tray.
- Sow perennial seeds straight away.
- Store annuals and biennials in a mouse-proof container and sow next spring.
- Consider starting a seed exchange with nearby gardeners.

5 Take Care of Dahlias

(late July)

DAHLIAS have evolved over the last 100 years from the grotesque dinner plates grown for the show bench to the exotic border belles they are today. Look after them in July and they will carry on flowering until the first frost. This could mean 4 months of non-stop flowers – something most plants could never manage.

The most important thing you can do at this time of year is dead-head them at least twice a week to prevent them setting seed. For if they do set seed they will stop flowering and stubbornly refuse to start again. Flower shape matters. Double varieties rarely set seed, but semi-doubles and singles do. If dead-heading is out of the question, opt for double fully-petalled varieties.

In many varieties the spent flower heads are large enough to be identified easily; they resemble triangular cones laid on their sides. However, in some varieties it's difficult to distinguish between the buds and the flowers that have gone over. Buds resemble round buns in shape, whilst the cone-shaped seed heads have a distinctive point and nearly always feel wet to the touch. Using small scissors, snip away any pointed potential seed heads.

Watering is also important. Try to avoid doing it in the evening, however, because this makes it easier for slugs and snails to mount an assault. They particularly enjoy the dark-leaved varieties. If you are going to feed, use a potash-rich plant food designed for tomatoes. This will keep the stems firm so that they support the flowers. Nitrogen and dahlias don't go together. They respond by becoming very leafy.

Did you know? The dahlia is unique because the seed from a single plant produces a variety of daughter plants with a kaleidoscope of flower types. The secret lies in its chromosomes – many dahlias are octoploid, with eight sets of chromosomes instead of the normal two, meaning that one plant holds much more variation than usual in its genetic make-up. Sowing dahlia seed is like doing the lottery – you never know what will pop up. So if you do find viable seed, sow it.

Organic Tip ✔

If a one-off frost threatens in September, cover your dahlias with a sheet of horticultural fleece, because it could be weeks before another frost occurs. Growing dahlias among hardier herbaceous plants also offers protection.

SECRETS OF SUCCESS

- Dahlias are Mexican plants and, like penstemons, tender salvias and tobacco plants, they seem to flower more enthusiastically from late summer onwards, once the evenings begin to draw in. So it's really worth dead-heading these plants in July to prolong their flowering season.
- Single and semi-double dahlia flowers attract bees and hoverflies. Their presence in a sunny border will help sustain these insects.

VARIETIES

For varieties, see March, page 45.

6 Cut Back Hardy Geraniums after Flowering

(late July)

LOTS OF hardy geraniums start flowering in May and June and by now they have begun to look ragged and their middles have become sparse. Cut them back now and they will put out new leaves in a matter of days, sometimes producing another crop of flowers. Plants that don't set seed often re-bloom profusely.

Other early-flowering hardy geraniums will have browned and may be setting seed. These include named forms of our meadow cranesbill (*Geranium pratense*) like 'Mrs Kendall Clark'. They need cutting back to prevent unwanted seedlings, although you could save some of the seeds if you wish for either February or March sowing. Certain sun-loving, low-growing varieties, including 'Mavis Simpson', 'Russell Prichard' and 'Coombland White', should be left alone, as they stay compact and keep flowering. These three fleshy-stemmed hardy geraniums tend to be short-lived, as they flower themselves out, so propagate regularly by dividing in spring. However, if you see a loose piece of stem, pull it away from the base now and pot it up.

Organic Tip ✔

Try not to have too many double flowers in the garden if you want to encourage wildlife. If the stamens and nectaries have been replaced with extra petals, the flowers are of little value to insects, which cannot collect sustaining pollen and nectar from them.

PLANTS THAT RESPOND TO A LATE-SUMMER CHOP

***Geranium* 'Orion' AGM**
The best blue-flowered sterile geranium of all. It will flower by May and then billow out into a large plant. Cut down now, and it will do it all again by late August.

***Geranium* 'Patricia' AGM**
A non-stop, black-eyed magenta sprawler with *G. psilostemon* blood. Makes a large sterile plant that is hardly ever out of flower.

***Geranium* 'Rozanne' AGM**
A sterile sprawler with mottled foliage and soft-blue flowers. At RHS Wisley they Chelsea chop it (see page 74) so that it is glorious in September. Or allow it to flower first and then chop it back now.

***Nepeta* 'Six Hills Giant'**
The ultimate sea of soft blue on a long-flowering, billowing plant. It begins in May, but if cut back now to nothing it will re-sprout and flower until late. A sterile plant.

***Anthemis* 'Susanna Mitchell'**
One of the longest-flowering plants in the garden. This sprawler produces masses of lemon daisies from early May. Cut down now for a later show. A sterile plant.

Did you know? Sterility (an inability to set seed) can be a good thing for the gardener because sterile plants tend to produce flower after flower in a vain attempt to reproduce. It happens more in some plants than others and hardy geraniums are one such group. Their flowers still attract pollinators. Closely related species often produce sterile offspring when they hybridize. Double-flowered plants are usually sterile because their stamens and style have been replaced by extra petals. As a result, they last longer in the garden and that is why plant breeders are wooed more by double flowers than singles.

SECRETS OF SUCCESS

- Don't be half-hearted when cutting back hardy geraniums or other plants. Most plants respond to a scalping by quickly forming new leaves. Hardy geraniums reduced to nothing will come back to life after a week.
- Leggy silvers can also be cut back now. These include all dianthus, rock roses, artemisias, anthemis and nepetas. Cut back to the lowest leaves.
- The one plant you must never cut back is the lupin, despite the fact that the foliage nearly always looks shabby in July; doing so will ruin next year's display.
- If you're unsure whether to snip or not, cut back half the plant, then stand back and observe. Even if that half doesn't bounce back quickly, it will have time enough to recover before autumn. *Knautia macedonica* (a wine-red scabious), for instance, really resents being chopped. It sulks for weeks.

AUGUST

August is an unforgiving month in the garden. Everything that's wrong shows now, with glaring accuracy, so this is a good month to make notes about the gap that's sprung up, or the appalling mismatch that stands out like a sore thumb.

Most gardens are lacklustre in August. It's partly the dry weather: often the water table is at its lowest now. It's also the light: it's as flattering as overhead neon on your complexion. Don't despair. Work on improvements for next year and wait for September – the most rejuvenating month of all. Quick fixes are allowed and one great container, well placed, can woo the eye from a tired area, making all the difference.

1 Get Out Your Notebooks

(early August)

INVEST IN two strong notebooks in bright colours, one pocket-sized and one large. Always have the small book with you when visiting gardens. Write the name of the garden and the date visited. Record the name of any plant you find particularly attractive, what you like about the garden in general and any other info. Take special notice of plant combinations that catch your eye. Try to visit and analyse a few new gardens every year. Find an excellent garden nearby that's open for much of the year. Make monthly visits, record them and you will learn a lot.

Use the larger book for your own garden. Divide the garden into areas and name each one. My own basic list includes the rose border, the snowdrop patch and the grass crescent. Label a double page for each area and get into the habit of recording your thoughts as soon as they occur to you, otherwise these insights are lost in time. On the left-hand page record what works: this is just as important as writing down problems. On the right-hand side make notes about any problems and their solutions. Plants may need dividing, they may need moving, they may not be earning their keep, or you may need more of them. Tackle the solutions in quieter moments and that way your gardening will have direction. It will improve. A photographic record also helps greatly.

Did you know? The late Christopher Lloyd of Great Dixter in East Sussex was drawn to visitors if they had a notebook and pencil in their hands. It marked them out as worth speaking to. He knew that if someone asked about a plant and didn't write down the information straight away it would be lost for most within minutes.

Organic Tip ✔

If you make a conscious effort to adopt the 'right plant, right place' style of gardening you will avoid plant diseases almost entirely. It is the key to natural gardening. This approach will also provide you with a garden for all seasons, although you must also embrace diversity by planting trees, shrubs, perennials, annuals, ferns, bulbs and grasses.

SECRETS OF SUCCESSFUL GARDENING

- Be true to yourself. Grow what you enjoy growing. Don't follow fashion.
- Be adventurous. Try new plants. However, try to choose plants that suit your conditions. If you try to grow something three times and fail, abandon ship! Tell yourself you never really wanted to grow it anyway!
- Recognize the value of foliage and where it should be planted. Silver foliage only works in full sun in well-drained positions: its sparkle flatters purples, pinks, blues and reds. Golden foliage lights up shade, but scorches in full sun. Blues, whites and yellows look jaunty among gold. Green foliage comes in hundreds of shades: it should be the mainstay of the garden.
- Use texture and shape, and seek out plants with a vertical presence to break up the mounds, otherwise the garden will look like a rumpled duvet. When blending flowers, look at the detail in every one – the purple veins of white geraniums, the orange stamens of pink potentillas. Pick up these details and exploit them.
- Value buds: they offer intricate form and texture and last much longer than flowers.

2 Frisk Roses for Black Spot

(early August)

THE MUGGY days of August create perfect conditions for the spread of fungal diseases like black spot (*Diplocarpon rosae*), so it's time to frisk your roses for those tell-tale marks on the leaves. Tidy up any fallen rose leaves lying on the ground before too many spores are released. Place them in the bin rather than on the compost heap. Examine the leaves on all rose bushes and remove any that look suspect. Affected leaves tend to turn yellow and develop black spots. Doing this now will keep this fungal disease to the minimum. If you can meticulously tidy up on a regular basis it will help break the cycle of spores being washed back up from the ground on to the foliage.

Another excellent way of preventing black spot is to under-plant your roses with a carpet of well-behaved perennials to act as a buffer zone. Violas, hardy geraniums and campanulas are amongst the most useful, as many have a gentle growth habit. Silver-leaved plants, like lavender, and dark-leaved sedums are also effective on sunnier edges. You can 'Chelsea chop' all of these plants (i.e., cut them back in late May) so that they produce a later crop of flowers to follow the June flush of roses (see page 74).

Good pruning helps to lessen black spot. Always prune so that there are spaces between each stem to improve the circulation of air. Remove any lower branches that graze the ground. If you have a rose that's a martyr to the disease, don't spray. Dig it up.

Did you know? The German rose-breeders Kordes have developed a series of disease-free roses over the last 40 years or so because most German gardeners will not use chemicals in their gardens. They breed only from healthy, disease-free roses. Their roses all have the breeding prefix KOR in the name printed after the rose's name.

Organic Tip ✔

Healthy, well-fed roses are like healthy, well-fed people. They are much less likely to succumb to disease. Feed your roses well (see page 97).

SECRETS OF SUCCESS

- Modern roses fit into the flower border very well and having plants growing around them helps to prevent black spot taking hold. The perennial foliage tends to act as a buffer zone.
- Remove badly affected roses and replant with healthier ones. To avoid rose sickness, dig out the old soil and replace it with new soil enriched with organic material.
- If you need to water your roses, make sure that the foliage stays dry. Carefully tip cans of water over the root. Adopt this technique with all mildew-prone plants too, including phloxes and monardas.

VARIETIES OF AWARD-WINNING KORDES ROSES

'Joie de Vivre' (Korfloci01) – Rose of the Year 2011
A compact, blush-pink floribunda.

'A Moment in Time' – Rose of the Year 2012
A bright-red compact floribunda with excellent foliage.

'Lancashire' (Korstegli)
Very double, small–medium-sized, warm red blooms borne in large trusses, in great profusion. Arching stems with rich, glossy green foliage. Can be used for ground cover.

'Welcome Home' (Koraubala)
Glossy green, disease-free foliage, with abundant medium-sized peach flowers and a light fragrance.

3 Take Clematis Cuttings

(mid-August)

IF YOU have a favourite clematis there's still time to take cuttings. Look for leafy shoots that are semi-ripe – not too soft or too woody. They should feel pliable yet firm. Cut a long shoot from the base and you should have a stem that has leaves every few inches or so. You need to cut the long stem into sections roughly 10cm (4in) each; the technique is to cut midway between each set of leaves, not straight underneath the leaves as with most plants. These are called internodal cuttings and the node (the point where the leaves emerge) should be in the middle.

Plunge ten to twelve cuttings into a 12.5cm (5in) pot almost filled with a 50:50 mixture of horticultural sand and compost. Water them well with tapwater that has been left to stand in a watering can for a day or so – this warms the water and releases chlorine. Place the cuttings in a cold frame and keep them cool and moist, or cover the pot with a polythene bag and stand it somewhere shady. If you can supply bottom heat, cuttings root more quickly. Keep the cuttings moist and check them regularly, removing any that show signs of mould, or those that die. Pot up into John Innes No. 1 once roots appear.

Some clematis cuttings are very difficult to root, even for professionals. Montanas are the easiest; viticellas vary from variety to variety; and spring-flowering Atragenes (including alpinas and macropetalas) always seem slower.

Did you know? The word 'clematis' is derived from the Greek *klema*, meaning vine branch or vine-like. Before the word 'klema-tis' was coined the whole genus was known as *Atragene*, meaning 'firecracker' in Greek. Apparently, when large dry stems of *Clematis vitalba* (old man's beard) are placed in a fire, the heat causes them to split, making a noise like firecrackers. The word is used now to describe the Atragene Group of clematis, containing around ten spring-flowering species and their offspring.

Organic Tip ✔

There's a clematis for every situation, but hardiness varies greatly. As a rule, evergreen clematis that flower in the first third of the year tend to need the shelter of a warm wall. Clematis flowering in April as the leaves appear (the Atragenes) are very hardy if they have good drainage. Montana clematis and C. orientalis *don't enjoy severe weather and therefore are never pruned hard. Viticella clematis, flowering in the second half of summer, are tough. These are cut back hard in spring* *(see page 40)**.*

SECRETS OF SUCCESS

- The best month to plant a clematis (so that it races away easily) is September.
- Prepare the site well and add organic matter. If planting close to a wall, position the clematis 1m (3ft) away if possible.
- Keep the roots cool. Place a slab over the roots, or put a container in front of the clematis to shade the ground if the planting site is sunny.
- If planting in spring or summer, water well until autumn.
- Support your clematis. Gripple (a self-tensioning-wire system) is the easiest to manage.
- Prune as instructed on the label.

VARIETIES

***Clematis* 'Betty Corning' AGM**
This has viticella blood, so it is cut back hard every spring. By July it will be covered in frilly, pagoda-shaped flowers in soft-gloaming shades that hover between lilac-pink and blue.

***Clematis* 'Princess Diana' AGM**
Rose-pink, tulip-shaped flowers in abundance. *C. texensis* blood and much easier than most tulip-flowered varieties.

***Clematis* 'Huldine' AGM**
Small pearl-white flowers, each lightly barred in violet-pink. The six even tepals are set round yellow-green stamens, so this clematis has a cool, translucent quality lacking in many whites. Each flower has an attractively darker back.

***Clematis* 'Arabella' AGM**
A modern scrambler that produces a long succession of mauve-blue flowers studded with white filaments and yellow stamens. Let it lollop over a bank or come up through low shrubs.

For further varieties, see March, page 42.

4 Trim English Lavender

(mid-August)

LAVENDERS come in three distinct types which vary in hardiness, so they are pruned accordingly. English lavender (*Lavandula angustifolia*) is the hardiest and longest-lived of all. It flowers in early summer and the stubby flower spikes are held on short stems a few inches above the narrow leaves. Varieties like 'Hidcote', 'Munstead' and 'Imperial Gem' are often used for hedging, as many have a compact habit. By August these lavenders are really over, so they should be pruned hard back to the base now so that they regenerate before winter. If pruned like this every year they will survive for 20 years or more.

The lavandins (*Lavandula × intermedia*) are in their full glory now. They have a billowing habit, with tall stems topped by slender, tapering flowers. They tend to be twice as tall as English lavenders and they form cloud-shaped plants. These hybrids of *L. angustifolia* × L. *latifolia* are less hardy and would not survive hard pruning, so they are trimmed back in September. Cut into the foliage, removing up to a third. Once clipped, they make wonderful roundels for winter interest. They have shorter lifespans than English lavender, lasting between 5 and 7 years on average.

Lavenders with tufted flowers topped by petals are the least hardy of all. They are often known as French or Spanish lavender. They have an upright, woody frame and often begin flowering in May. Allow this first flush of flower to finish, then cut them back by a third in July. Their average lifespan is 5 years. Take cuttings of lavandins and Spanish lavender between May and mid-August (see page 81).

Did you know? Lavender used to be known as 'spikenard' (from *naardus*, after the Syrian city of Naarda). It was used in the Holy Land to make an expensive, soothing balm. In the Gospel of St Luke (the most informative of the four) Mary anoints the feet of Jesus using a pound of ointment of spikenard. However, spikenard is also a common name of *Nardostachys grandifolia*, one of the great spices of India. In classical literature it and lavender were often confused.

Organic Tip ✔

If you want to cut English lavender to dry the flowers, it needs to be snipped in Wimbledon fortnight, in the latter half of June and into early July. Leave some flowers on the plant, though, because lavender nectar is highly concentrated and bees adore it.

LAVENDERS

***Lavandula* x *intermedia* 'Grosso'**
The bright-blue lavandin grown around Provence for its sharp, aromatic oil. Tight, tapering flowers radiate from greenish foliage.

***L. angustifolia* 'Melissa Lilac'**
Extra-large, pale-lavender flowers held in darker calices make this one of the prettiest English lavenders. A sumptuous plant.

***Lavandula* 'Regal Splendour'**
A New Zealand variety that manages to come through most winters, with a dark, fat middle topped by a wavy cascade of veined purple bracts.

***L. pedunculata* subsp. *pedunculata* AGM**
Very long, wavy bracts set above the flowers – which add movement and charm to any sunny border. Commonly known as Spanish lavender

SECRETS OF SUCCESS

- All lavenders have silvered, aromatic foliage and this indicates that they need full sun and good drainage.
- Once established, lavenders can survive on very little water. They do so by developing a deep root system, but obviously this takes time. When you plant new lavenders they will need watering for their first season.
- Get to know your lavenders. Compact English lavenders are perfect for border edging and hedges. Billowing lavandins make statement plants with their swirl of foliage and long stems.
- The most variable group are the tufted lavenders known as French or Spanish. They vary in habit, stature and flower colour.
- Buy from lavender specialists. They have a vast range.
- Handle and fondle your lavender: it's a great stress-buster.

5 Cut Yew and Beech

(*late August*)

AUGUST is the best month to begin tackling yew and beech hedges so that they look gloriously trim in winter. Both make excellent hedges because they can cope with a once-a-year trim. Beech hedges cut now will retain some leaves throughout winter, providing extra shelter for bird and insect life. The russet foliage will look attractive in winter light. Leave some leaf litter at the base of the hedge as well, if possible.

Yew can be sappy. If you are using shears (for topiary, for instance), a bucket of water, scrubbing brush and a cloth are useful.

Immerse the blades in water, scrub and wipe with a damp cloth regularly – this helps you to get a clean cut. It's also useful to lay down a large sheet or tarpaulin to catch the clippings. Always try to cut yew and all conifers on a dull day, or when the foliage has a covering of dew, to prevent sun scorch. Feed with blood, fish and bone after cutting.

If you have a young hedge, trim the side shoots back, leaving the base wider than the top to allow light to reach the base. Resist the urge to lop the top until the desired height is reached, as an unlopped yew hedge can put on 38cm (15in) of growth a year. Contrary to popular opion a yew hedge doesn't take a lifetime and, in the early stages, trimming two or three times during the growing season makes the hedge much bushier. Plant bare-root yew between November and March, leaving 45cm (18in) gaps.

Did you know? The oldest yew tree in Britain is to be found at Fortingall in Perthshire. It is at least 3,000 and maybe even as many as 5,000 years old. In 1769 its girth measured over 17m (56ft). It may live another 1,000 years yet.

Organic Tip ✔

Yew produces red fruits with a fleshy, edible covering that is adored by thrushes and blackbirds. All other parts of the plant are toxic, but it is probably a myth that the trees were planted to deter grazing animals from entering the churchyard. Historians now tend to the view that many yew trees found in churchyards pre-date the building they supposedly guard; in fact, the churches were built next to them. They may have marked religious sites long before Christianity arrived.

SECRETS OF SUCCESS WITH YEW

- The fact that yew trees can live to be thousands of years old convinces gardeners that establishing a yew hedge will take for ever. However, you can produce a good yew hedge within a few years if you nurture it.
- Plant your new hedge in enriched soil, forming a single line with 45cm (18in) between plants. Bare-root plants should be planted between November and early March. Containerized trees can be planted in autumn or spring.
- The chief advantage of yew is that it can be cut back to bare wood and still sprout. It also tolerates deep shade.
- Feed and water your new hedge in the growing season – between April and August. Water on seaweed fertilizer or a nitrogen-rich plant food.
- Remember not to cut the top off your yew hedge until it has reached the correct height. If you trim the top it will branch out and take much longer. Just cut the sides two or three times during the growing season, leaving the base wider than the top to allow light to reach the entire hedge. Most young hedges should be cut like this – not straight down.
- Once the desired height is reached, trim the top a little, then keep working on the sides, cutting back two or three times a year until it is thick enough.

YEWS

Taxus baccata **AGM**
Our plain green native yew tree makes the best hedging.

T. baccata **'Semperaurea' AGM**
A golden form of yew that can be used for a hedge, although it tends to be slower growing than the green yew.

T. baccata **'Fastigiata' AGM**
The columnar, upright, slim variety often used for topiary. Not suitable for hedging.

6 Think about Bulbs

(late August)

I KNOW it seems like the middle of summer, but it's time to think about spring-flowering bulbs. Try to buy them now. The choice is greatest and the bulbs have only just left storage, so they will be in the peak of condition. Store them somewhere cool until planting time. Most can be planted at the beginning of September, including ornamental alliums, narcissi, muscari, snowdrops, crocus, scilla and hyacinths. They will start into growth quickly and develop good roots. When choosing, be aware that in general yellow varieties of narcissi flower earlier than white and cream ones.

Tulips are the exception: they are planted from November onwards because they suffer from a fungal disease called tulip fire (*Botrytis tulipae*). Cooler conditions discourage the disease (see page 160). It's generally best to buy later varieties, which follow the majority of daffodils. Late-April Triumph tulips and May-flowering varieties will lift the late-spring garden and most of the really excellent varieties flower then.

When choosing bulbs, try to select excellent varieties with AGM awards. Restrict yourself to a few varieties and plant those in fifties or hundreds. They are cheaper to buy in quantity (rather than in sixes) and a spread of one variety is much more pleasing to look at than lots of little groups of different kinds.

Did you know? Greek legend tells us that the goddess Persephone was abducted by Hades, god of the Underworld. She was picking white daffodils when he approached her, but his touch turned all the flowers bright yellow. It was also said that they grew on the banks of one of the rivers flowing through the Underworld. The Greeks called these *asphodel* (flowers of the dead) and daffodil is a corruption of that word.

SECRETS OF SUCCESS

- Segregate May-flowering tulips and narcissi from earlier-flowering varieties so that the spent flowers don't spoil later displays.
- Concentrate on planting large numbers of just a few varieties to avoid the 'sprinkles on the trifle' look.
- Randomly scatter them to get a natural effect. Don't plant in straight lines.
- Plant to twice the depth of the bulbs.
- When planting bulbs in containers, it's easier and more effective to use one variety per container. Then they all flower and fade at once.
- Allow the foliage to die down naturally if you intend your bulbs to naturalize.
- Bulbs are treated with fungicide, so wash you hands after handling or wear gloves.

Organic Tip ✔

When planting treated hyacinths for indoor use, grow a selection of the same variety in small, individual pots. It's then possible to pick three or four at the same stage and pot those up together in larger bulb bowls.

BULBS

***Scilla siberica* AGM**
Cobalt-blue bells 10cm (4in) high that bring miniature daffodils to life. Moderate self-seeder and good in shade.

***Crocus* 'Vanguard' AGM**
An elegant, silver-grey and lilac-purple, large-flowered crocus that pre-empts the other larger-flowered Dutch crocus by 2 weeks – hence its name.

***Narcissus poeticus* var. *recurvus* AGM**
The Pheasant's Eye narcissus, with fragrant, single white flowers and a yellow eye edged in red. One of the last to flower, but dainty, delicate and willowy.

***Hyacinthus orientalis* 'Delft Blue' AGM**
A warm blue hyacinth for a sweet scent. You can plant ordinary bulbs for spring displays; however, if you want Christmas blooms, buy treated bulbs and plant them in early September. Keep them in the dark for 10–12 weeks.

SEPTEMBER

September is a stunning month. The even light in the northern hemisphere makes the whole show come to life, giving the garden a jewel-box richness. The bulk of the work is done and there's time to enjoy life as autumn dews revive the garden.

*Tender plants come into their own, helped by even day length; they will soldier on until the first frost strikes. They lend an ornate presence, for plants from sunnier climes have pigment-packed petals. New England asters (*Aster novae-angliae*) sparkle now and, if September is warm, clouds of butterflies dance in attendance. In all, September gives May a good run for the Best Month of the Year award!*

1 Nurture the Butterflies

(early September)

GARDENING should be a sensuous affair and butterflies are a true delight. Their numbers are declining, however, and every gardener should help by providing a supply of their favourite nectar-rich plants in return for the aerobatic spectacle early September usually brings. If you do, you will attract the high-speed Painted Lady, the low-flying Small Tortoiseshell and the basking Peacock.

Access is a big problem for butterflies encumbered with large wings: they can't scramble down a narrow trumpet as the smaller bee can. Instead they seek out level platforms on which they can land. Luckily, the daisy is perfect and it reigns supreme in September. The central disc consists of hundreds of tiny flowers and all are full of nectar – the sugar-rich energy drink butterflies need to fly.

The stiff-stemmed New England asters (*A. novae-angliae*) flower in September just when most butterflies are about. These rugged plants, with mainly pink, lavender or purple flowers, form large clumps which lure butterflies in. Small Tortoiseshells adore them. Fortunately New England asters endure well with little attention, unlike the more-demanding New York asters (*A. novi-belgii*), which need very moist conditions in order to avoid mildew and also require regular division in spring. Echinaceas and rudbeckias are also highly popular with butterflies.

Flat-topped flowers also attract them. *Verbena bonariensis*, the willowy perennial verbena, which can reach chest height or more, is another favourite and it carries on producing its mauve flowers until October at least. This self-supporting plant can be used among dahlias: it is rigid enough to act as a staking system and far more attractive than canes.

Did you know? Nectar varies greatly in strength. Marjoram (*Origanum vulgare*) was found to contain 76 per cent sugar, the highest level, as opposed to crown imperial (*Fritillaria imperialis*) with only 8 per cent. Bees and butterflies select plants producing sugar-rich nectar. Plants can also turn their nectar on and off. *Saponaria officinalis*, or soapwort, has pallid flowers that are pollinated by moths, so it turns on its nectar tap from late afternoon onwards. *Anchusa azurea*, or bugloss, produces its small blue flowers in a loose panicle. It switches nectar flow on and off randomly, forcing bees to search (and so pollinate) every flower.

BUTTERFLY PLANTS FOR EARLY AUTUMN

***Verbena bonariensis* AGM (Perennial Verbena)**
Tall and willowy verbena with a long presence. The shorter *Verbena rigida* (30 cm/12in) is also excellent and a brighter purple. Painted Ladies bask on mine.

***Origanum laevigatum* 'Herrenhausen' AGM (Marjoram)**
More of an August butterfly plant – but a tremendous lure, with neat, dark foliage and sprays of two-tone pink and purple flowers. Last year my plants had thirty-six Small Tortoiseshell butterflies on them all at the same time.

***Centranthus ruber* (Red Valerian)**
A cottage garden favourite that will flower for ever if dead-headed and cut back. Irresistible! Very good for the Hummingbird Hawk moth.

***Aster novae-angliae* 'Barr's Pink' (New England Aster)**
One of many you could grow. This one is a striking lilac-pink.

Organic Tip ✔

Nectar and pollen are important in gardens. They provide the energy and protein, respectively, that insects need to feed and breed. Flower colour often indicates a plant's main pollinator. Blues, pinks and purples seem universally attractive to bees. Pallid whites, silver-pinks and yellows usually attract moths. Flies are drawn to green and white flowers and the tiny flowers of umbellifers suit their small mouth parts. Hoverflies love yellow and orange. Grow a range of flower shapes, from saucer to trumpet and from snapdragon to upturned umbrella, to attract the widest range of insects to your garden.

SECRETS OF SUCCESS

- Nectar flows only in warm conditions, so don't plant anything in a cold position if it needs pollinating.
- Afternoon sunshine is highly valuable later in the year. Plant your butterfly magnets where they will catch it.
- Windy gardens need a shelter belt. A native British hedge is the most eco-friendly (see page 155).
- Fallen fruit is a butterfly lure – plums are adored by many.
- Buddlejas are the ultimate favourite for butterflies (see page 57).

2 Autumn Maintenance

(early September)

REMOVE perennial rosettes (like dandelions and plantains) from areas of lawn you wish to look pristine. Repair any damage now. If you need to create a new lawn, early to mid-September is the best time to sow grass seed as long as the ground is damp enough. The daytime and soil temperatures are still warm enough to ensure good germination.

The technique varies according to the size of the area. If you are restoring existing worn turf or seeding small areas you can generally get away with distressing the surface with a short-tined rake or fork, treading it down and then scattering the seeds. Water well, cover with wire netting and keep off the area for 6 weeks. The ground should be kept watered throughout this time, but shouldn't get waterlogged.

For larger areas, or if you are creating a new lawn from scratch, ground preparation is a must. Rotavate the area if possible, or dig it through by hand, removing any stones and all weeds. Either add organic material to poor soil, or add grit or sand to heavy clay. Leave the ground to settle for 10 days , then hoe off any emerging weeds. Then sow the seeds as instructed on the packet (see page 29).

Certain plants need to be cut down now so that they form a tight cushion of fresh growth. This will allow them to overwinter successfully. Shear off achilleas, perennial violas (including all *Viola cornuta* varieties) and lychnis, plus anything else that looks leggy and thin at the bottom. Leave penstemons and most silvers intact until next spring.

Did you know? Don't despair about clay soil: it is fertile and it delivers nutrients gradually over a long time. Great Dixter has clay to contend with, but it is improved during winter by adding lots of 3–5mm coarse grit. This stays in the soil for years. Never stand on wet soil. Use a plank, or two planks. Making mounds for planting improves drainage and gives the water somewhere to go in wet weather.

SECRETS OF SUCCESS

- Cutting down in September requires common sense. Anything that's borderline-hardy (including penstemons) must be left alone now. The top growth will protect it in winter weather.
- Straggly hardy plants need attention now. They are not going to survive winter unless they have tight growth at the crown, so trim them back. They will have weeks to toughen up before winter arrives.
- Move and divide early-flowering perennials if your soil is well drained. Those on clay should wait for spring.
- Leave autumn-flowering plants until next spring.
- Trim back or tie in any wall plants that may become damaged in autumn gales.

PLANTS THAT WILL NEED A HAIRCUT

Viola cornuta

These charming violas (for dappled-shade) produce wispy, pansy-shaped flowers in May and late summer. They are one of the most attractive plants to grow under roses or in flower-filled borders. They need two haircuts a year and, if given these, they will survive in the garden for decades. Cut them back hard, to the ground, after their first flush in May and they will flower again on straggly growth. Cut them back now in September, to the ground again, and they will form a mat of bright-green leaves capable of resisting winter.

***Helianthemum nummularium* (Rock Roses)**

These sprawling plants are summer-flowering and by now most varieties have gone leggy. Trim them back hard so that they overwinter. They make good edgings on sunny borders.

Organic Tip ✔

If you have clay soil that gets cold and sticky, all your planting and division is much better done in spring than autumn. That way new plants won't sit in cold, claggy soil.

3 Begin to Wind Down the Garden

(*mid-September*)

SUMMER nights are long behind us and soon autumn gales and harder weather will arrive. Garden paraphernalia should be given some loving attention now, then stored over winter. Seats and tables can be wiped down and treated with a suitable preservative. Umbrellas and their stands should go away, but they must be completely dry. Watering cans, always vulnerable if water freezes inside, need emptying and storing. Any wicker baskets, pottery cane covers, cushions and garden ornaments should also be stored in the shed.

Don't put the whole garden to bed, however. A totally bare affair looks awful and it's bad news for wildlife. Leave as many late-summer perennials and grasses as you can to catch the light and frost (see page 22).

Do tidy any areas of spring bulbs whilst they are either dormant or in the early stages of growth. Once spring begins to arrive these areas cannot be trampled on without damaging emerging bulbs, so it is an autumn job.

Do also tidy (as much as possible) any borders containing structural evergreens like box or yew, then these green sentinels can shine alone and really lift the garden. Remove any canes no longer needed. Give the lawn edges an extra-special tidy, because by mid-October most mowing will have ceased. Book an autumn service for your mower now to avoid the hectic spring rush. Finally, enjoy every last vestige of summer – sometimes there are odd days in late October that gladden the heart.

SECRETS OF SUCCESS

- Areas of long grass provide shelter for insects and small animals. They also encourage brown butterflies to breed in your garden, provided you have the correct species of grasses. The Gatekeeper, a small brown butterfly with pretty orange markings, uses several grasses such as fescues and meadow grass. Eggs are laid on the grass in late summer and the young caterpillars hibernate in the base of grassy clumps. Willow or hazel hoops can be woven round these areas to make them look as though they should be there – just look at Highgrove. At this time of year you need to lift the hoops and mow off the long grass.
- The value to wildlife of the untouched corner cannot be stressed enough. Allow leaves to lie in these areas and consider planting bird-friendly teasels to attract a charm of goldfinches.
- Grow evergreen herbaceous plants and shrubs to provide cover. Many pulmonarias keep their leaves and most biennials (like foxgloves and hollyhocks) have rosettes of leaf that endure through winter.
- Plant winter-green ferns and ivies now for evergreen touches. They will have plenty of time to get their toes into the warm soil.

Did you know? The daffodil produces its flower spike by Christmas and the bud waits just under the soil surface for warmer temperatures before it emerges. So if it's a cold spring, the first daffodil may be very late. Crocus behave differently, however. They are tempted into flower by light, so they can bloom in sun-baked spots even in cold January.

Organic Tip ✔

September is a month when slugs and snails often return in numbers and they seem to lay a lot of eggs now. Disturbing the soil disrupts them, so hoe bare patches of ground whenever possible so that eggs surface. Birds will eat them. Do not use slug pellets — young hedgehogs are about.

4 Plant Clematis and Other Climbers

(mid-September)

THE SECOND half of September is the best time to establish a climbing clematis. Clematis can be used in a variety of ways and they take up little ground room, so every gardener should grow plenty. They can be used up walls and trees, through roses, and over shrubs. Vigour and spread vary, so do check with an expert supplier so that the clematis matches the support rather than overwhelms it.

Clematis like a cool root run, so if you want one to scramble over a large shrub, plant it on the north-facing aspect out of midday sun. Prepare a hole that's much bigger than the root ball, break up the ground at the bottom and sprinkle in some bonemeal. Add some coarse grit if you're on wet clay. Bury the lowest leaf joints and cover with 5cm (2in) of soil. Always water any newly planted clematis thoroughly.

Other container-grown climbers can also be planted now. The walls of your house and garden offer sheltered microclimates, but don't plant right up against them. Try to allow at least 60cm (2ft) between plant and masonry – more if possible. Always enrich the soil so that it's rich in humus and able to retain water in this dry position.

WALL SHRUBS AND CLIMBERS FOR NORTH, SOUTH, EAST AND WEST

***Pyracantha* 'Orange Glow' AGM (Firethorn)**
Thorny evergreen with dark shiny foliage and large clusters of orange berries. Trim in May or June. A toughie for an east-facing wall.

***Magnolia grandiflora* 'Victoria' AGM (Bull Bay)**
This leathery-leaved, evergreen magnolia has a red indumentum (covering of fine hairs on the underside of the leaves) which picks up the red bud scales. Lemon-scented, ivory-white flowers follow. This is a hardy Canadian selection and it's lime-tolerant. For a sheltered west or south wall. Up to 15m (50ft).

***Garrya elliptica* 'James Roof' AGM (Silk Tassel Bush)**
Large, evergreen wall shrub bearing grey-green tassels from January. Pollution-tolerant and suited to coastal conditions. Best on a north wall.

***Ceanothus* 'Puget Blue' AGM (Californian Lilac)**
An evergreen variety, one of the bluest, and an excellent wall shrub for a sunny, south-facing wall. Trim back after flowering.

For clematis varieties, see May, page 66.

SECRETS OF SUCCESS WITH WALLS

- South-facing walls are effectively giant storage heaters, soaking up the warmth of the midday sun and rationing it out. They protect tender plants that couldn't survive elsewhere and they should be fully exploited.
- North-facing walls sound horribly chilly. However, in most areas of Britain they can be surprisingly sheltered from prevailing winds and wintry weather. These sunless areas are perfect for shade-loving evergreens and Asian twiners.
- East-facing walls catch the early-morning sun. This can cause a destructive thaw after a frosty night, leading to browned flowers. Avoid putting spring-flowering camellias and magnolias in this position. East-facing walls also bear the brunt of searing April winds, so this is a challenging aspect best left to 'toughies'.
- West-facing walls are usually the gentlest: they pick up ambient south-westerly winds and Atlantic moisture. Plants are bathed in evening sunshine during summer, but avoid scorching midday heat.
- If you have a long expanse of wall there will be significant differences along that stretch. A south-facing wall meeting an east-facing wall is likely to be harsher than the west-facing corner of the same wall. Similarly, the western edge of a north-facing wall will get evening sunshine during the longer days of June, July and August. The north-eastern corner will be drier and bleaker.

Did you know? Not all clematis climb. Some herbaceous types sprawl and these make effective plants in herbaceous borders. In September the star of the show is *Clematis heracleifolia*, with small, fragrant, starry blue flowers that turn up at the edges.

Organic Tip ✔

Experienced growers buy their clematis whenever they see them, but they don't plant them into the ground. Instead they pot them up into much larger plastic pots and nurture them through summer. They water them copiously, because clematis are thirsty plants, and feed them with a high-potash food: tomato fertilizer or rose food are both acceptable. Then they plant them in September and the plants romp away. This method avoids planting in dry conditions and leads to fewer losses.

5 Take Cuttings of Roses

(late September)

THE SECOND half of September is the best time to take hardwood cuttings of shrub roses, hybrid teas, floribundas, rambling roses, vigorous climbers and all species roses. Choose this season's growth, making sure that the selected stems are pencil-thick and firm to the touch. Ideally, cuttings should measure 15–20cm (6–8in) in length.

Trim just underneath a leaf bud, remove all the leaves and damage the stem at the lowest joints, or eyes, so that you weaken the cambium layer (the layer of actively dividing tissue) just below the surface. This will encourage faster rooting. Dip the bottom 5cm (2in) into hormone rooting powder. Cuttings can be planted into deep pots of gritty compost; however, a slit trench in a sheltered position outside is more usual. Cut into the ground with a spade and push the soil apart, then fill the bottom of the slit trench with gritty sand. Place the cuttings so that they are submerged along a third of their length. All cuttings should shoot in the following spring, but should be left *in situ* for a further 12 months.

September is also a good time to plant container-grown roses. However, bare-root roses, which are delivered between November and March, are less expensive and the range is often greater if they are ordered now.

Did you know? Some roses shine in September, among them the hybrid musk roses bred by Joseph Pemberton (1852–1926), an Essex vicar. Pemberton raised twenty-four hybrid musk varieties, nine of which have 'taken their place at the forefront of roses', to quote the late rosarian Graham Stuart Thomas. These nine widely acclaimed roses are very diverse: they include reds, whites, copper-pinks, silver-pinks, creams, yellows and apricots. Their habits vary from lax to upright to widely arching, yet they share several wonderful characteristics, including scent, health and vigour. They bear clusters of flowers held in darker buds.

Organic Tip ✔

Roses with long arching branches do not like being pruned hard. Reduce the leaders by a third.

SECRETS OF SUCCESS WITH ROSES

- Good husbandry.
- Follow a careful three-stage feeding regime: potash in February and rose fertilizer in April and July (see page 97).
- Provide fertile, deep soil. Roses enjoy clay.
- Pray for summer rain.
- Dead-head perpetual and repeat-flowering varieties.
- Prune appropriately (see page 24).

VARIETIES OF HYBRID MUSK ROSES

'Penelope' AGM
Perhaps the best hybrid musk Pemberton raised. Free-flowering, semi-double blooms held in clusters. They open a creamy pink and fade to creamy white. Good coral-pink hips.

'Cornelia' AGM
Small, dark leaves frame copper-apricot flowers which fade to a light coppery pink. Very good in autumn.

'Felicia' AGM
Upright and vigorous with silver-pink flowers opening from long dark buds. Good as a hedge.

'Buff Beauty' AGM
Not bred by Pemberton, but descended from his line. A graceful, arching, medium-sized bush with bronzed foliage and warm apricot flowers.

6 Store Frost-tender Plants and Protect Succulents

(late September)

ALLOW LARGE containers of lilies, agapanthus and other vulnerable plants to dry out by cutting down on watering, and also stop feeding them now. This will improve their chances of surviving winter. In 4 weeks' time, once dry, they can be placed under the bench of an unheated greenhouse and left well alone until next spring. If you have to store them outside, place them in the lee of a building, on the driest side – usually north or east. You can also carefully lay the pots on their sides: this prevents rain from penetrating the crown of the plants.

Lilies can be top-dressed, re-potted or placed in the garden, depending on how long they have been in the same pot. Varieties normally perform well for 2 years. After that, remove the top 5cm (2in) of compost and add a nutrient-rich John Innes No. 3. Bulbs in their third year really need to be replaced.

Check succulents in pots (echeverias and aeoniums, etc.) in case of vine weevil. Start by giving the plants a tug – often an infected plant comes away where the stem meets the roots. Up-end the pot and check for gaps in the root system – this often indicates weevil damage too. If all looks well, place the pot in an unheated greenhouse. Pull off leaves and small rosettes for cuttings and allow these to dry for a couple of days, before plunging them into sand or a 50:50 compost and sand mixture.

Try not to store leggy, old pelargoniums or other tender plants. Take cuttings instead. Hide the cuttings of the tenderest plants, like plectranthus and solenostemon (formerly coleus), among those of hardier pelargoniums. Invest in a fleece blanket – they're invaluable in cold weather. Most things survive if kept dry under a double layer.

Did you know? All vine weevils are female and look like a speckled ridged beetle. In late summer they lay their eggs close to certain plants, each adult producing an average of 500–600 eggs. The grubs live on roots but the adults eat leaves, leaving characteristic crescent-shaped holes on leaf edges. The adults are nocturnal and even though they cannot fly they can often climb up walls towards electric lights. Nursery owners take an evening stroll and kill them on sight.

Organic Tip ✔

Vine weevil grubs like soft-stemmed plants, including primroses, heucheras, succulents and sedums. They also like soft, peaty compost and the craze for container-planting in peaty compost has led to an increase in numbers. Gardeners can limit the damage by using coarse grit. Mix it with soil-based compost like John Innes (equal parts) when potting up and you will get fewer problems. Topping each pot with more sharp gravel seems to help too.

SECRETS OF SUCCESS

- In summer, evergreen shrubs like skimmias and laurel often show weevil damage. Semicircular bites can be seen round the edge of the leaves and this should act as a warning of their presence.
- Winter will not kill off the weevils' white larvae – they have their own built-in antifreeze.
- Tug the stems of all plants in the greenhouse and examine vulnerable plants in the garden – those with soft, fleshy stems. Heucheras, sedums and primroses should be regularly divided to prevent fleshy stems protruding from the ground. Top-dress with gritty compost.
- If you intend to overwinter a container of soft-stemmed tender plants, early September is the key time to use nematodes that control vine weevil. These should be watered on in the late afternoon (after the container has been well watered), preferably on a warm day. This gives the nematodes the best chance of penetrating the compost and attacking the weevil larvae. Once the weevils have been dealt with, the number of nematodes will fall back naturally.

OCTOBER

October is a bonus, as the days can be warm and the sun hazy. There may be the odd frost, so a fleece blanket applied when a frost is due usually rescues the situation for another 3 or 4 weeks. Admittedly the dahlia stems are getting floppy (due to lack of light and cool conditions), but they still continue to dazzle in soft autumn light.

It's important to have late flowers to sustain the bees for as long as possible, so keep the garden going. The preponderance of golden-yellows gives any rich, dark-red flowers an ornate presence, like garnets in an old gold Victorian ring.

1 Plant Biennial Wallflowers

ENJOY October, but also focus on next spring and plant some biennial wallflowers. They should be available in garden centres now, as year-old, spring-grown, bare-root plants. These easily grown biennials provide important winter leaf. The fragrant flowers, with the scent of Parma violets, appear just as the later tulips bloom. The two make perfect partners in a sunny border, or in a container, and when warm spring sunshine arrives you'll be able to drink in the fragrance of these insect-friendly flowers.

Biennial wallflowers (usually labelled *Cheiranthus*) have been a garden favourite for centuries and many old varieties can still be found. However, in recent years new breeding has produced an F1 Sunset Series which comes in pastel apricot, primrose, cream and more-vibrant orange, purple and red. This British-bred series excelled in the RHS wallflower trial held between 2003 and 2004. Seeds containing a mixture of colours are available for April and May sowing, and these vigorous, branching hybrids are also sold fully grown in spring. It is also possible to buy plug plants of the Sunset Series. After flowering, these plants need removing.

There are also perennial wallflowers, many of which produce flowers from May until October. These are labelled *Erysimum* and, if dead-headed, can make a real difference to a sunny garden. Good varieties include 'Constant Cheer' (a Jacob's-coat combination of mauve, orange and yellow), 'Bowles' Mauve' AGM and 'Orange Flame'. These perennial types are not nearly as strongly scented as the biennials, however.

VARIETIES OF BIENNIAL WALLFLOWER

'Scarlet Bedder'
An old, blood-red variety. Fragrant.

'Persian Carpet'
A soft mixture of reds, creams, yellows and oranges. Fragrant.

'Aurora'
A sunset shade of subdued pink. Fragrant.

Siberian wallflowers
These flower in May and they are squatter and less fragrant. Their colour range is limited to orange, apricot or yellow.

Did you know? Wallflowers were given this name as they often flowered in the lee of a warm wall. Robert Herrick (1591–1674), the Cavalier poet, wrote about how the wallflower came to be, describing a tragic incident involving a fourteenth-century Scottish noblewoman, Elizabeth, daughter of the Earl of March. Her father wanted her to marry the future king of Scotland, the heir to Robert III, but unfortunately she had already fallen in love with Scott of Tushielaw, a young nobleman from a rival clan. The strong-willed Elizabeth refused to obey her father, who had her locked up in the tower of Neidpath Castle on the banks of the River Tweed. Her handsome suitor disguised himself as a minstrel and serenaded her whilst they made plans to elope. When the time came, however, Elizabeth fell from the tower to her death, landing close to a flower growing beside the tower's wall. The broken-hearted Scott set off to wander through the land wearing a sprig of this flower, which subsequently became known as the wallflower. It still symbolized faithful devotion in Victorian times.

Up she got upon a wall,
Tempting down to slide withal:
But the silken twist untied,
So she fell, and, bruis'd, she died.

Organic Tip ✔

Wallflowers, members of the cabbage family, need good drainage and warm sun – a family trait. Warmth will make the nectar flow, improving the fragrance. The biennials are the really scented ones.

SECRETS OF SUCCESS

- When growing your own wallflowers, sow the seeds in April in warm rather than hot positions.
- Prick out seedlings into individual pots.
- Once the young plants are 10cm (4in) high, pinch out the tops so that they bush out. When they reach the same height again, pinch them out a second time.
- Cuttings can be taken from the perennial varieties (*Erysimum*) in early summer.
- It is also a good idea to cut perennial Erysimums back in June or July, after their first main flush of flower is over. This keeps them compact and extends their life.

2 Leaves: to Rake or Not to Rake?

(early October)

DON'T IMAGINE that you have to gather up every single leaf in your garden. Leave any that are under shrubs, hedges or in woodland borders to rot down naturally. This dry layer is important: it's the protective duvet of the natural world and it will accommodate hibernating insects, including ladybirds, as well as spiders, small mammals and amphibians.

However, you will need to gather up any leaves that are on the lawn, or any that are smothering sun-loving silver plants. Invest in a rubber-tined rake to collect them from borders, lawns, gravelled drives and patios. It will make quick work of the job and it's so much quieter than a leaf vacuum!

If you have only a few leaves you can add them to the compost heap. However, if you have masses you will have to make a dedicated heap, or collect them in black bags. They are a valuable resource because they rot down to produce a friable substance called leaf mould. The problem is the decomposition process takes a long time and involves fungi that thrive in cool, damp conditions.

If you have enough room, make a square wire frame for a dedicated 'leaf heap'. In 18 months' time you will have crumbly leaf mould which can be added to compost or used as a top-dressing or mulch. Those of you with limited space can make leaf mould by collecting damp leaves in black plastic dustbin sacks. Keep some air in the bag, then gently puncture the sides so that air can aid the decomposition process. Store the bags for at least 18 months, then tip the contents out and use the brown crumbly mixture in the usual way.

SECRETS OF SUCCESS

- Patience is needed to make good leaf mould.
- Certain leaves are slower at producing leaf litter: these include hazel, beech, oak and hornbeam. Others (like sycamore, horse chestnut and lime) are much faster.
- Black fungal spots and leaf miners are diseases and pests specific to particular trees and will not affect other plants in your garden.
- Leaves absorb pollutants, so don't collect them from busy streets.
- Keep the pile of leaves damp, turning it occasionally to improve friability.

Did you know? Some leaves are high in carbon and low in nutrients, which is why they take a long time to rot down. Once rotted, the nutrient levels of leaf mould are low, but it makes an excellent soil conditioner or mulch.

Organic Tip ✔

Collect your leaves on a damp day and they will rot down much faster. Mow them if they are on lawns: this will chop them up and help to speed the decomposition process. A mixture of chopped leaves and lawn mowings can go straight on to the compost heap.

PLANTS THAT ADORE LEAF LITTER

Wood anemones (*Anemone nemorosa*)
Gentle, spring-flowering woodlanders with nodding pale flowers.

Trilliums (Wood Lilies)
The North American woodlanders that appear as the snow melts in their native land. They need moisture – a mulch of leaf mould is ideal.

Snowdrops (*Galanthus*)
Early-spring bulbs that multiply well in friable soil top-dressed with home-made leaf mould.

Bluebell (*Hyacinthoides non-scripta*)
The British native bluebell flowers in late April or very early May. This elegant plant has gently arching stems of violet-blue flowers all held to one side of the stem.

3 Plant a Winter Container

(mid-October)

USE ONE of your rugged wooden or frost-proof terracotta containers to plant up some winter foliage. Place it close to a doorway and it will delight you when you go in and out for the next 3 months. Your arrangement should last for at least 2 years. After that, relegate the plants to the garden.

Leave one or two small gaps in the foliage and plug them with a series of small pots. Pansies, primroses, snowdrops, crocus, scillas, small reticulate iris, Christmas roses and miniature daffodils all make useful highlights. As soon as their flowers fade, replace them with something else.

Rich green foliage is the most effective in winter because it looks warm and welcoming. It flatters white flowers. Good evergreen, compact shrubs include *Sarcococca confusa* and *Skimmia* × *confusa* 'Kew Green'. Winter-green ferns can be used; polypodiums and polystichums both keep their fronds until spring. Plain green ivies, vincas and pachysandra are also suitable. Tuck white Christmas roses among the rich greens; they will flower in December and January.

Golden-leaved ivies and shrubs cast their own light and shade, making ideal arrangements in shadier conditions. The touches of gold make blue and purple bulbs more vibrant. They will also flatter miniature daffodils once they become available.

Cooler cream-and-green variegated ivies add elegance to white Christmas roses. You can also make a smoky combination using plum-toned heucheras and × heucherellas with brown, spiky grasses.

SECRETS OF SUCCESS

- When you go to buy plants, be creative. Don't go with a shopping list made in advance. Select plants and arrange them in the trolley, ensuring that they mix together well.
- Look for one fabulous key plant, then for suitable supporters with different foliage textures – making sure that the foliage tones together.
- Choose only plants at the peak of perfection. One shabby plant will spoil the whole arrangement.
- Pack the plants in tightly – it will look much better. A

45cm (18in) wide container will need about nine permanent plants.
- Always include one grass (or grass-like plant) to create a jagged line and use trailing ivies to soften the edges of the container.

Did you know? Evergreen plants have always been seen as potent miracle-workers. Holly trees were often planted close to houses to protect against lightning, poisoning and negative spirits.

Organic Tip ✔

When potting up a large container, move it into position first, then stand it on pot feet to encourage better drainage. This is really important in winter. Use a loam-based compost like John Innes No. 2 or 3; it will deliver nutrients over many weeks and it is heavy, so your pot will be more stable.

WINNING COMBINATIONS

***Ophiopogon planiscapus* 'Nigrescens' and red flowers**
This grass-like plant has black leaves, soadds drama to all red flowers. Start with cyclamen: they are plentiful now. If they catch the frost, replace them with red primroses.

***Carex comans* Bronze Form, x *Heucherella* 'Sweet Tea' and small-flowered orange winter-flowering pansies**
A smouldering swirl of fine leaf supported by marmalade, shawl-shaped foliage with sparky small pansies.

Variegated green-and-cream ivy with Christmas roses (*Helleborus niger*)
An elegant and cool mixture. You can add white cyclamen.

Green-and-yellow ivy with yellow and blue flowers
This crisp, pretty arrangement needs a good golden-splashed ivy. The flowers can be changed – begin with pansies and primroses, followed by miniature yellow and blue bulbs.

4 Divide and Move Peonies

(mid-October)

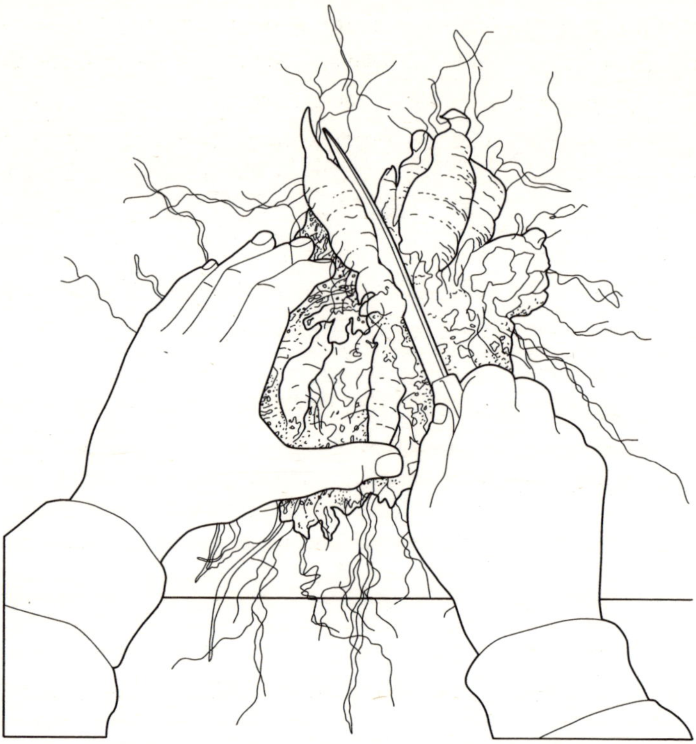

THERE IS an old wives' tail that herbaceous peonies cannot be moved, but this is entirely wrong. These adaptable, long-lived plants transplant well and early October is the best time to tackle the job. It's also the best time to plant new varieties. The most garden-worthy are the *Paeonia lactiflora* varieties. Their blooms last longer than cottage garden peonies (*P. officinalis*) and they flower later, just pre-empting roses. The woody stems should be cut back as they fade, in October, and general fertilizer should be sprinkled around the plants. Feed them again in March.

They key thing with peonies is not to plant too deeply. The top of the crown should be 5cm (2in) below the soil surface and all pot-grown peonies should be carefully planted so that the soil level in the pot matches the level in the garden. Planting too deeply causes poor flowering. If you have a clump in a sunny position that isn't flowering well, it probably needs raising.

New varieties can be ordered now; bare-root plants are dispatched between October and March. Plant as soon as possible in frost-free ground. The tuberous roots need reasonable drainage. If you are on clay, incorporate coarse grit. If your soil is thin and poor, add organic matter (such as well-rotted compost) when planting. Single peonies tolerate more shade.

Dividing a large clump needs to be tackled with a pruning saw once the foliage starts to die down. Lift and clear away the soil. Remove any dead wood and cut the plant into pieces containing roughly five buds each, then replant and feed.

Did you know? The peony has always been considered a potent plant. The Greeks thought it was really a god called Paeon whom Pluto had changed into a plant to keep him from being killed. Pliny writes that peonies should be dug only at night. If dug in daylight, a woodpecker would peck out your eyes.

Organic Tip ✔

Peonies contain toxic chemicals which deter most pests. Aphids leave them alone, for example. The only disease you are likely to meet is peony blight in wet springs. Infected leaves and buds turn brown, wilt and finally collapse. Cut off and dispose of infected plant material.

SECRETS OF SUCCESS

- Peonies need fertile, deep, moisture-retentive soil and summer rain. Water in dry conditions.
- If your soil is particularly heavy or sandy, mulch lightly with well-rotted manure or compost. Mulch around the peony, but avoid covering the top of the crown or it may become too deeply buried.
- Stake with hoop-like metal supports to prevent the flowers from flopping on the ground if heavy rain strikes.
- Dead-head varieties after flowering. Species peonies can be left to self-seed once the plants are established.
- Cut down dead foliage to ground level in autumn and clear it away. Top-dress with a handful of bonemeal or general fertilizer. Feed them again in spring.
- If your soil is acidic, an occasional top-dressing with lime will prove beneficial.

VARIETIES

'Duchesse de Nemours' AGM
A lemon-scented, creamy white with fine glossy foliage and real poise.

'Festiva Maxima' AGM
Pink buds which open to blush-white. Each bloom is studded with magenta flecks.

'Shirley Temple'
Excellent garden peony, with pale-pink double flowers that fade to cool white.

'Felix Crousse' AGM
Very prolific, with scented, double, magenta-purple flowers.

5 Plant Bare-root Hedging, Trees and Roses

WE ARE now at the beginning of the bare-root season, when ornamental trees, hedging whips, fruit trees and roses can be planted in their dormant, leafless state. Although they arrive looking like bare sticks, there are several advantages to buying a field-grown, bare-root specimen rather than a container-grown one. A bare-root plant is often cheaper, the range of varieties is often greater and bare-root plants rarely look back once spring arrives. Bare-root plants adapt to your conditions more easily too.

When planting time comes, improve the soil by adding garden compost or very well-rotted manure. Many roses have a graft or bud union that looks gnarled and bumpy. This should be positioned 7.5cm (3in) below the soil surface. Sometimes long roots can prove difficult to plant. Don't be afraid to trim them back as you spread them out. Carefully back-fill, then tread lightly in. Water well.

Trees are often grafted, but it's possible to see where the tree left the ground by looking at the trunk. Just replant to that level. If you intend to plant lots of ornamental or productive fruit trees, bare-root specimens are far cheaper and easier. However, you will need to water well in their first growing season.

Did you know? Before the advent of the plastic pot (in the 1960s) every commercially grown woody plant was sent out bare-rooted when dormant and planted between November and March.

Organic Tip ✔

Order from a reputable specialist nursery. It's important to stake trees as you plant, so get a tree tie and stake from the same source. If rabbits or deer abound, buy a tree guard too. Keep the weeds at bay: this makes a huge difference in the early years of a plant's life. Keep an area around the young tree free of grass and weeds: they out-compete the tree for nutrients.

SECRETS OF SUCCESS

- Prepare the ground before the plants are delivered and cover it with fleece to keep it frost-free.
- Open the packet as soon as it arrives and check the contents.
- Roses are always bundled together and a bunch of four looks like one, so do unsnip the string.
- Never plant in frosty conditions. Either make a slit trench in a sheltered spot by putting the spade in at a 45-degree angle and levering the soil apart. Lay the plants in to halfway up the stems. Or you can store roses or trees, etc. in the bag in a cool, frost-free place for a few days before planting.

6 Weed Your Paths

(late October)

THE GARDEN is winding down for the year, but there are lots of minor jobs that can be tackled now in order to save precious time next year. Turn your attention to paving and paths. Cooling temperatures and autumn rains will have prompted weed seedlings to appear in the cracks of paths and in gravel. These are still small enough to get rid of quickly and they will be more of a menace by next spring.

Paths become more prominent as winter arrives, as does the rest of the garden landscape, so this is the time to spruce up gates and drives, etc.

There are chemical products for treating weeds in paths. However, as a no-chemical, organic gardener I prefer to hoe and rake gravel to dislodge seedlings. If you invest in a cobra-headed hand tool it's easy to rake out the weeds from the small cracks in paving. Long-handled weeders for cracks and crevices are also on offer. Pull up any flowering weeds you spot in out-of-the-way corners.

The other organic way of dealing with weeds is to scorch them off with a gas-fired flame-gun. This can work well on gravel in dry weather, but the foliage has to be dry and deep-rooted weeds like dandelions can re-sprout.

Weed rosettes in lawns are also clearly visible now and easier to lever up than in the summer. Target dandelions to prevent them flowering next April.

Did you know? Dandelion flowers are a rich source of nectar for insects and the seeds are eaten by many birds, so in a wilder area of the garden they could be allowed to thrive. Bear in mind that one flower contains an average of 180 seeds and just one plant may produce between 2,000 and 12,000. These wind-dispersed parachutes often travel almost a mile from the parent plant.

Organic Tip ✔

Never walk past a flowering weed: pull it up. As the old adage says, one year's seed is seven years' weed – and that's optimistic.

SECRETS OF SUCCESS

- Getting on top of weeds is all about being tenacious and consistent.
- If you can make a huge effort on the weeding front by early May, things slow down again until late August when shorter, cooler days encourage germination.
- Hoeing is a vital way of getting rid of annual weeds.
- Perennial weeds need a lot of getting rid of – so don't give up.
- If an area is really badly affected by perennial weeds, you may be tempted to use a very effective weedkiller called glyphosate. It affects a vital metabolic process in plants called the shikimic acid pathway which animals do not have. But new research has found that the wetting agents used in commercial formulations are toxic to newts, toads and frogs. If you must use it, be very careful. It is not an organic treatment.
- Remember that regular weeding is therapeutic.

NOVEMBER

November is not a spectacular month in the garden: it tends to be damp and drear. However, if the sun shines and you've planted some tall grasses, they will help to lift the atmosphere, creating movement and form as the sun sinks ever lower. The trees have lost their leaves and their silhouettes, against a winter-red sky, can be stunning.

*You can almost sense the tug-of-war going on between autumn and winter. Sparkling frosts will pull you one way, but then you'll notice a last vestige of summer – perhaps a lone rose trying to defy the elements. By the end of the month winter will be king. A few fresh flowers will lighten your load: the yellow stars of the winter jasmine (*Jasminum nudiflorum*) and the hyacinth scent from the lanky viburnum 'Dawn' both begin to open in this rather bleak month.*

1 Plant Tulips

(early November)

EARLY November is an excellent time to start thinking about planting your tulip bulbs, but do wait for the temperatures to drop first. Don't do it in warm, clement weather because tulips are prone to a fungal disease called tulip blight or tulip fire (*Botrytis tulipae*) which is more likely to flourish in warm conditions. Planting can take place right up until Christmas without problems as long as the soil is frost-free. Your tulips will still flower.

Tulip blight symptoms can vary from bulb rot to grey-green lesions on the leaves, and may even result in spotted petals on badly affected plants. If you see this, remove and destroy the whole plant, but don't add it to the compost heap. Discourage the disease by removing tulips after flowering (if possible), or plant them in different places. If the disease strikes you will have to leave the ground to recover and usually that means 5 years.

The most colourful tulips are the late-April-flowering Triumphs – a group bred and grown in Holland for the cut-flower trade. Excellent varieties include the dark chrysanthemum-crimson 'Jan Reus', the purple-veined white 'Shirley' and the beetroot-purple 'Negrita'. But they come in a wide rainbow of colours. Use the Triumph with May-flowering types to extend the season, but do select a colour scheme.

Did you know? Some tulip species grow wild around the Mediterranean basin but most can be found in the Caucasus and mountainous areas of central Asia such as Pamir Alai, the Hindu Kush and Tien Shan. There might be as many as 100 species, but many are variable and they hybridize freely. Scientists think the genus *Tulipa* is evolving rapidly.

SECRETS OF SUCCESS

- Plant at twice the depth of the bulb or deeper. Between 10 and 15cm (4 and 6in) is ideal.
- When selecting varieties, don't go for a hundreds-and-thousands, multicoloured look by planting small numbers of different varieties. Buy fifties or hundreds and stick to three varieties in each recipe. Then mix all three together. This is much more effective and cheaper too.
- Concentrate on later-flowering tulips: these follow on from most daffodils, rather than competing with them, and flower in late April and the first half of May.
- Always use one variety of Triumph tulip with May-flowering types so that you get at least 4 weeks of interest. May-flowering varieties include parrot, fringed, single-late, double-late and viridiflora. All have their own distinctive shapes. Mix the heights too so that you avoid a flat, tabletop look (see Varieties below).
- Add some spring bedding – such as wallflowers or myosotis – to large pots of tulips to give a frame for the tulips.
- You can leave tulips in the ground after flowering and they will return for 2 or 3 years. These bulbs produce smaller flowers, and if you plant new ones among them, the mix of flower sizes creates a charmingly natural look.
- If leaving tulips in the ground, remove the stalk and leave just one large leaf. This should allow the bulb to regenerate.

Organic Tip ✔

Avoid buying tulip bulbs with specks of blue mould. Discard any you find. In order to prevent disease, all commercial bulbs are treated with a fungicide, so wash your hands after handling them and, if you have sensitive skin, wear gloves when planting. Organically certified bulbs are available in small numbers.

VARIETIES

'Red Shine' AGM
A classic, lily-flowered tulip with outward-turning petals in shades of ruby-red. Up to 55cm (22in).

'Recreado'
A single-late tulip with egg-shaped, doge-purple flowers. 50cm (20in).

'Black Hero'
This double form of 'Queen of Night' forms black, artichoke-shaped blooms that shrug off wet weather. 60cm (2ft).

'Spring Green' AGM
An ivory-white tulip with green, feathered petals. Superb in shade. 50cm (20in).

2 Lift and Store Dahlias

FOR MANY years gardeners have left their dahlia tubers in the ground and got away with it. However, the recent brutal winters have caused extensive losses, so it's best to err on the side of caution and dig your tubers up. The technique is simple enough. Once the plants become blackened and frosted, carefully lift them with a fork, then cut the stems back to 5cm (2in) long. Label them as you lift them. Clean up the tubers, removing any fibrous roots or soft tubers; these can be cut out cleanly. Wash the tubers thoroughly with the garden hose to remove soil and any slugs or slug eggs. Dry them off somewhere cool so that the tubers are dry, clean and firm. At this stage you can treat them with a fungicide like yellow sulphur powder if you wish, although I prefer not to.

Once the tubers are dry, find a dark, frost-free place to store them by laying them out. A shed or a garage can be ideal, but the temperature should remain under 5°C (40°F). Check them regularly throughout the winter. Don't let them shrivel up. A plastic tray with holes is ideal, but if storing in a shed try to keep the excess cold out. A polystyrene sheet and a blanket should do the trick.

Did you know? Dahlias first arrived in Europe from the high plains of Mexico towards the end of the eighteenth century. They were considered at first to be a vegetable because their tubers were similar to potatoes. The Spanish tried to feed them to cattle and to humans, but both declined to eat them.

SECRETS OF SUCCESS

- The key to successful storage is cleaning the tubers thoroughly and then drying them off.
- Unheated basements and cellars make ideal storage areas, but sheds also work well as long as frost can't penetrate the tubers. You also need to protect them from rats and mice.
- Check your tubers weekly and discard any that are rotting.
- Handle the tubers very carefully in early spring to avoid damaging the young shoots.
- Start them off in March in a warm place.

Organic Tip ✔

The thorough washing process is key to storing dahlias. If the tubers are covered in dry soil, this attracts moisture in storage. Once they are clean, dry them off really well for 2 or 3 days. Drain and dry the tubers upside down so that any water in the hollow stems drips out.

VARIETIES

For varieties, see March, page 45.

3 Tie In and Train Rambling Roses

(mid–late November)

TIE IN and prune once-and-only-flowering rambling roses before winter gales set in and damage them. The new olive-green stems (produced this year) are easy to see and still supple enough to bend without snapping. As winter progresses, these pliable stems will toughen up and become brittle. Pliability is important when training roses, because bending the stems slows down the sap and this encourages more flowers. For this reason new stems can be coiled round upright wooden supports, or woven through a pergola, looped along a fence or trained horizontally rather than being allowed to go straight up into the air.

Choose a still day and arm yourself with a pruning saw and sharp secateurs. Protect your arms with thick clothing and use goggles too. Always start by removing the 3 Ds – diseased, dying or dead wood. Then create an open shape by removing any stems that cut across each other: this improves air flow and lessens the plant's vulnerbility to disease. This is a general procedure for all rose-pruning.

With ramblers the aim is to remove one in three of the older stems from the base and replace them with new ones. Tie in the new stems securely, using rubber-coated Soft-Tie. Reduce any lateral growth if you need to. Ramblers are vigorous and disease-free, and they drip with flower in June. Partner them with a viticella clematis (like the purple 'Étoile Violette') for extra late-summer colour.

Did you know? 'Rambling Rector' is a very old rambler, often called 'Shakespeare's Musk', although the Bard probably meant *Rosa moschata*. It will cover a large area and produce clusters of creamy-white, button-shaped flowers in June. These are adored by bees.

VARIETIES

'Sander's White' AGM
Well-behaved, clean-white rambler that will flower in shade. Always the last to flower, so useful for extending the main rose flush. A once-and-only rose. Up to 3.6m (12ft).

'Vielchenblau' AGM
This blue-violet rose is superb on stone walls. It looks faded and it smoulders in summer sun. A once-and-only rose. Up to 4.5m (15ft).

'Bobbie James' AGM
A white, tree-covering scrambler with large cupped flowers. A once-and-only rose with a sky's-the-limit tendency. Up to 9m (30ft).

'Phyllis Bide' AGM
A repeat-flowering, soft-salmon-pink and yellow rambler with thorny stems and semi-double flowers. Up to 3.6m (12ft).

SECRETS OF SUCCESS

- Ramblers are easy to grow. They tolerate poor soil and their simple breeding often makes them resistant to common diseases like black spot.
- Most flower only once, so there is no dead-heading.
- They can be used to clothe pillars and fences to great effect. They can also scramble through trees and cover buildings. Select the right variety for the job.

Organic Tip ✔

Ramblers vary in vigour, so it's important to select the correct one. 'Kiftsgate', for instance, is a thug. It has killed six beech trees in the Gloucestershire garden after which it was named. Describe your space and position to a rose nursery and then ask for suggestions.

4 Check Over Trees

(late November)

WHEN TREES are in leaf it's very difficult to check over the wood. Now that many are dormant, it's a good time to look at them carefully for damage. Take off any damaged wood, anything that looks as though it's dying and any diseased wood. Check the trunks of mature trees and make sure there are no lesions or splits. It's difficult to repair these, but they callus over in time. However, being aware helps to highlight future problems with diseases.

Younger trees should be securely staked, so check the area close to the tree stake and loosen the tie if necessary. Once a tree has been in the ground for a few years the stake and tie can be removed. Weed around newly planted trees and, if the soil is unfrozen, you could use a mulch mat. These are carpet-like circles that fit round trees.

Also look at the silhouette. The ideal shape for most trees is an open one, but different trees have different habits and profiles. Study the tree before making any cuts. Hard pruning now will invigorate the tree and encourage a rapid response in spring. New upright shoots, known as water sprouts, will appear. These are leafy shoots that don't bear fruit or flower and they shade the tree and inhibit proper development.

Did you know? Knocking on wood for luck has ancient origins: our ancestors summoned protective spirits from the trees by rapping on the trunks.

SECRETS OF SUCCESS

- Generally trees that flower and fruit need gentle pruning that will promote both and will also improve the tree's strength. So remove only the dead, diseased and dying wood and tip the branches. Take out any crossing wood and open up the canopy to allow the light to penetrate. Try to develop a strong tree framework.Keep the canopy open.
- Check trunks and tree ties throughout the year.
- Remove tree stakes after 3–4 years.
- If you have to re-stake, angle in the stake at 45 degrees so that the end going into the soil is well away from the main roots.

Organic Tip ✔

Don't think that everything has to be pruned. Avoid pruning magnolias and hamamelis unless they need it. Also avoid pruning daphnes: they are capricious enough as it is. Don't prune in severe weather: it will stress the tree further and may let in disease.

TREES FOR WINTER EFFECT

***Betula utilis* var. *jacquemontii* 'Doorenbos' AGM (Himalayan Birch)**
These white-stemmed birches weave a special magic and their black twiggy canopy creates a sharp contrast. They need fairly good drainage. This clone is superb.

***Acer* x *conspicuum* 'Phoenix' (Phoenix Maple)**
A choice small tree worth chasing. The striated bark turns an orange-red in winter.

***Prunus serrula* AGM (Tibetan Cherry)**
With a mahogany trunk polished up to a high-gloss finish, this small tree has an open canopy of branches that support simple white cherry blossom.

***Acer griseum* AGM (Paperbark Maple)**
The shaggy, cinnamon-brown bark will warm up any winter's day and this acer is easier to grow than many. When buying any acer, try to find an excellent specimen – even if it does cost more.

DECEMBER

December is a watershed month, because after the winter solstice – two-thirds of the way through this month – the days begin to lengthen again. After that point the gardener's spirit rejoices once more. By mid-January snowdrops, daphne and hamamelis will brighten our lives – and it's only a matter of weeks away.

Evergreens woo the eye now and, if your garden is flat and uninteresting, these rich green plants will solve the problem. We may even get snow, which makes a winter wonderland of any garden. We may be trapped inside but the birdlife will continue to brighten our lives. This is the month when the view from the window becomes so important.

1 Look After Your Birds and Insects

THE NATURAL food in the hedgerows has dwindled now and, as more and more migrant birds arrive on British soil, it's time to set up a bird feeder or two if you haven't done so already. It's vital to feed your garden birds in winter and smaller birds suffer most. But it's also a window-watching occupation that makes the garden as interesting now as in high summer.

Next spring your garden's resident birdlife will reward you by removing lots of your pests to feed themselves and their broods. The blue tit collects scale insects, aphids, leaf miner grubs and small caterpillars. An average brood needs 10,000 invertebrates in the 3 weeks between hatching and fledging. So these creatures do a terrific job. Even seed-eating birds have to collect invertebrates for their nestlings. They will pick the aphids from trees and roses and gobble up the gooseberry sawfly larvae. This year I watched a chaffinch pick a gooseberry bush clean of sawfly caterpillars.

Set up your feeders in a quiet area of the garden close to trees, so that birds can fly to and fro. Most activity takes place in the first hours of daylight and an hour or two before dusk, so replenish the feeders at midday if possible. Try not to spill seeds and nuts on the ground, as spillages attract rodents.

Black sunflower seeds are appreciated by finches, including winter immigrants like bramblings, blackcaps and siskins. The tit family prefers peanuts, but woodpeckers also love them. Chaffinches usually feed on the ground. Fat balls provide the greatest energy boost and a supply of water is also an essential.

Did you know? One ladybird will eat fifty aphids per day. A female will lay 1,500 eggs between April and July (possibly later). These hungry babies start off in their larval stage by eating their mustard-yellow egg cases, then go on to aphids. They shed their skin four times before pupating. When a seven-spot adult emerges from its pupal case it has no spots at first: they develop a few hours later. Most ladybird species produce one generation per year and these need to hibernate over winter before they become sexually mature and able to breed.

Organic Tip ✔

Do not kill aphids with insecticides. They will sustain baby birds and there are lots of predators scouting for aphid colonies next to which they can lay their eggs, including hoverflies, lacewings and ladybirds. There are many tiny parasitoid wasps that lay a single egg inside an aphid. The lava eats its host from the inside and after a fortnight or so emerges as an adult through a small neat hole in the aphid's abdomen. Even 'organic' sprays (like mustard and soft soap) will kill these predators and parasitoids.

SECRETS OF SUCCESS

- Provide a source of water for your garden birds, especially when the weather is freezing.
- Fill up feeders regularly.
- Offer a variety of food, from fat balls to sunflower seeds and peanuts.
- Also put out fatty scraps on the bird table.
- In heavy snow, clear a square metre of ground on which birds can feed.
- Raisins, suet and old cheese are all gratefully received.

2 Cut Off Hellebore Leaves

(early–mid-December)

IT'S A GOOD idea to cut away the foliage of hybrid hellebores (*Helleborus × hybridus*) destined to flower in February and early March. This solves two problems – mice and hellebore black spot disease.

Mice tend to hide under the leaves and are very partial to the buds, so removing the leaves discourages them and makes them more visible to predators.

Taking off all the leaves also helps to prevent a fungal disease caused by *Microsphaeropsis hellebori*, which causes dark patches to develop on their foliage. Removing the leaves prevents the spores being splashed back from the soil on to the new leaves produced in early spring.

There is another upside to this task. When the flowers appear they will be clearly visible, the fresh foliage framing them beautifully without any ragged old leaves being present.

Cutting the foliage back now needs careful footwork if you are to avoid precious bulbs that lie just underneath the soil. Sprinkling a handful of gravel over your bulbs after they have flowered in late spring (while you can still see them) acts as a warning that the ground should not be disturbed. The gravel should be still visible now and is so much more pleasing to the eye than a forest of labels.

If you have a serious woodland garden, it is worth making a stepping-stone path through it. These stones do not detract from the display and are mainly hidden in spring. However, in winter the area is still dormant and you can walk through and maintain it without harming emerging woodlanders and bulbs.

Organic Tip ✓

Keep an eye out for the deadly Hellebore virus commonly called black death, which looks entirely different from black spot. It causes the plant to become stunted, deformed and marked by black streaks and ring patterns. The disease starts with black streaks like veins on the leaves. There is no cure, so destroy any affected plants.

Did you know? Hellebores are prone to aphid attack very early in the year and this may be how viruses spread – including the black death (see above). If you spot any diseased foliage cut it away and put it in the bin.

SECRETS OF SUCCESS

- All hellebore foliage should be binned rather than added to the compost heap, because black spot is widespread and you could perpetuate it in home-made compost.
- Be vigilant. Keep an eye out for blackened or partially blackened leaves and cut them off immediately.
- Mulch your hellebores with bark in autumn. This protective layer should help prevent spores being splashed back to the plant.

VARIETIES

For Hellebore hybrids and species, see May, page 74.

3 Provide Winter Red Berries and Fruit

(late December)

NO OTHER colour lights up the winter garden as effectively as red. Every garden should contain some berrying or fruiting shrubs to add the magic touch. A plentiful supply of red berries and fruit will also attract fieldfares, redwings, thrushes and blackbirds, and their acrobatic feats as they pluck the fruit always provides an entertaining diversion. These are birds that find bird tables and feeders difficult.

Red seems to draw birds like a magnet, but there is an order of preference. Holly berries generally disappear by the second half of December and it's always a challenge to remember to cut your Christmas sprigs before the birds devour them. The red-fruited crab apple, *Malus × robusta* 'Red Sentinel', is eaten only in hard winters, so it shines for much longer. Similarly, the tree-like *Cotoneaster frigidus* 'Cornubia' drips with clusters of red fruit and the 'Watereri' hybrid sold under this name hangs on to its leaves too. Or you could plant the downy-leaved, shorter *Cotoneaster lacteus* for its evergreen leaves and smaller clusters of berries. Often the berries on these shrubs last into early spring.

Organic Tip ✔

Holly berries and all other berries store well in cool conditions for several days. However, if growing holly for berries, it is only the female varieties that produce them: the males provide pollen. In country districts there's plenty of pollen, but you may need to plant a male in cities. One male can service a harem of females.

Did you know? Red has a remarkable ability to bring drabber colours to life. The famous watercolourist J. M. W. Turner (1775–1851) exploited this, using a splash of red to add vibrancy to moody shipwrecks and seascapes in muted colours. In a vision of sea green, grey and subtle blues a tiny red buoy in the foreground brings a work of art to life. This technique can be used in the garden in every season. A single pot of ruby-red, lily-flowered tulip 'Red Shine' in spring, or a red crocosmia like 'Lucifer', or a spattering of red crab apples on *Malus* × *robusta* 'Red Sentinel' can all have the same effect.

SECRETS OF SUCCESS

- In order to get berries on trees and shrubs there has to be pollination and this is more likely to happen in a sunny, warm position than in deep shade.
- Prune in spring, after berries or fruits have gone.
- Some berrying shrubs are dioecious – they have male and female flowers on separate plants. Check if this is the case and plant both if need be.
- If growing holly, use a specialist nursery because only a few varieties are stocked by garden centres.

RED-FRUITING TREES AND SHRUBS

***Berberis* 'Georgei' AGM**
Tiny translucent berries held in clusters arranged like bunches of grapes appear by late summer. This evergreen shrub is also sterile, so there are no unwanted seedlings.

***Malus* x *robusta* 'Red Sentinel' AGM**
A healthy crab apple with bright-red, oval fruits.

***Ilex aquifolium* 'Madame Briot' AGM**
A prickly French holly with jaunty butter-yellow and green leaves topped with vivid red berries. Dates from before 1866.

***Ilex* x *altaclerensis* 'Golden King' AGM**
The last red holly berry to be eaten by the birds, this rounder-leaved Highclere holly has smooth-edged, two-tone green leaves edged with a broad, irregular band of custard-yellow. Not a heavy berrier, but it can be clipped. Dates from 1858. Female, in spite of its name.

4 Protect Plants from Winter Weather

(late December)

WINTER OFTEN strikes in December, but many plants welcome a cold period of dormancy so that they can rest. Among these are fruit trees, tulips, peonies and roses. Other plants, deciduous perennials, for instance, retreat underground.

Mediterranean plants are more vulnerable and they could be protected with horticultural fleece. This is an effective way to shield them from damaging frosts. Bulbous summer-flowering plants are also vulnerable, but a layer of bark (over agapanthus, for instance) helps to insulate them. Other plants (like evergreen kniphofias) suffer severe damage. Although they may look ragged, resist the urge to tidy them until late March.

Remove any early snowfall from evergreens: these suffer greatly under the weight of snow. See also January, page 4.

Organic Tip ✔

If a favourite shrub gets a snapped branch, do some first aid. Find a 2.5cm (1in) bandage and a small splint, and tie and fix the bandage round the damage. Add a layer of Vaseline and use canes to support the branch.

SECRETS OF SUCCESS

- Keeping evergreens in good fettle in winter is easier with closely clipped topiary. Smarten it up in late August with a gentle clip and it will be compact enough to stop the snow from getting inside.
- Non-clipped evergreens should be planted in sheltered places where wind and snow are unlikely to damage them too much.

TREES AND SHRUBS FOR WINTER FOLIAGE

***Ilex* x *altaclerensis* 'Belgica Aurea' AGM (syn. 'Silver Sentinel')**
This statuesque, round-leaved holly forms a conical tree and each dark-green leaf is edged in rich yellow, to varying degrees. Large, orange-red berries follow.

***Ilex* x *altaclerensis* 'Camelliifolia' AGM**
A pyramidal tree with almost spineless, purple-toned, dark-green foliage and substantial red berries. Very glossy and green.

***Choisya ternata* AGM**
A rounded shrub with whorls of leaf for a sheltered position. Fragrant clusters of white flowers follow in summer.

***Aucuba japonica* 'Rozannie' AGM**
Aucubas are underrated shrubs that grow easily and quickly, reaching roughly 1m (3ft) in height. 'Rozannie' has serrated, rich green foliage and glossy red berries in winter. It's self-fertile so it will berry on its own.

INDEX

Val Bourne has been a fanatical gardener since the age of five. In her twenties she worked in vegetable research, at a lowly level, and she has always grown her own fruit and vegetables organically. She now has a large allotment, and fruit and vegetable patches amongst her extensive flower garden in the Cotswolds.

An award-winning writer, Val also serves on two RHS panels – dahlias and herbaceous and tender plants, which meet fortnightly to assess plants for the Award of Garden Merit (AGM). She lectures all over the UK and has also lectured in Japan and South Africa. Val writes regularly for the *Daily Telegraph*, *Saga* magazine, *Oxford Times*, *Grow It* and the Hardy Plant Society magazine. She also contributes to the RHS *The Garden*, and *The Rose Magazine*, amongst other publications.

She is the author of six other books, including *The Natural Gardener* (winner of the Gardening Writers' Guild Practical Book of the Year), *The Winter Garden*, *Colour in the Garden* and *Seeds of Wisdom*, as well as *The Ten-Minute Gardener's Vegetable-Growing Diary* and *The Ten-Minute Gardener's Fruit-Growing Diary*.

Her passion is still gardening!